©2023 Jamie Hecker

ISBN 979-8-9890404-0-7

Cover photo – Disney Legends Plaza at The Walt Disney Company headquarters in Burbank, California, by Jamie Hecker

# DISNEY LEGENDS

## MAKERS OF MAGIC

### VOLUME 1

JAMIE HECKER

# DEDICATION

This book is dedicated to my wife Suzanne, who unconditionally supports my forays into Disney research and writing.

It's also dedicated to the broader Disney historical community, particularly the late Jim Korkis, the men and women who professionally work tirelessly to research and document the many layers of the corporate and brand history of The Walt Disney Company and its many business ventures.

# ABOUT THE AUTHOR

Jamie Hecker was raised in Indiana and is an academically trained historian. He attended Purdue University, where he earned a Bachelor of Arts degree in US History. He writes for Celebrations magazine, (celebrationspress.com), where he focuses on Disney Legends, the men and women who have made significant contributions to The Walt Disney Company. Learn more about his work at https://jamieheckerwriter.com

# THE DISNEY LEGENDS

# FOREWORD

As a teenager growing up in the 1980s, I was already passionate about Disney history. As soon as I managed to learn enough English to allow me to do, I sought out American magazines which contained good, accessible books and articles about Disney history. Two of the writers whose work I loved were Jim Korkis and Jim Fanning. My understanding of Disney history did not yet run very deep and I needed historians to gently guide me in this gigantic maze of stories about Disney artists and their creations. In other words, the two Jims provided well-written, entry-level pieces about the men and women who made Disney "Disney" and about their fascinating creations.

Thanks to them I discovered who was who, how their operated and how they collaborated. I also learned much more about their boss, the great Walt Disney. The two Jims took me by the hand and helped me understand the big picture, which, years later meant that I was able to dig much deeper and to finally become an actual Disney historian. Without them and without their work, I would never have acquired the fundamental Disney history knowledge that would one day allow me to write Disneyland Paris—From Sketch to Reality, Disney's Grand Tour, The Origins of Walt Disney's True-Life Adventures or the They Drew as They Pleased—The Hidden Art of Disney art book series.

It is therefore with delight that I discovered the work of Jamie Hecker in the pages of the magazine Celebrations. His profiles of Disney Legends go beyond the short biographies released on the D23 website but are short enough to provide great introductions to the lives and work of these exceptional artists for readers who love Disney history but have yet to become Disney history specialists.

Like Jim Korkis' and Jim Fanning's pieces, Jamie's articles are well-written, well-researched and a joy to read.

It is therefore with enthusiasm that I see some of them collected in this first volume of what I hope will become a long book series.

One, which, I suspect, will inspire quite a few teenagers to one day become Disney historians.

Didier Ghez
Coral Gables, September 2023

# PREFACE

If you were to spend an ample amount of time with me, you'd come to find out that my bookcase is primarily stocked with Disney books and magazines. If you were to take a closer look, one of the books is my first foray into Disney non-fiction. If you were to flip through the ten plus years of Celebrations magazine I have, you'd see plenty of articles and columns I've written.

You'd also see from my college diploma on the wall that I'm an amateur historian, academically trained at Purdue University with a BA in US History, 1988. American history in general is fascinating, and Disney history is my specialty.

If you spent event more time with me, you'd discover I'm a cat person, with Tasha and Millie ruling the house. I like dogs too, particularly when they belong to someone else. A special thanks to Tucker and Fancy, my sisters-in-law's adorable canines. When I visit my brother, I also get to meet Eddie, the wonder dog.

After enough time with me, you'd eventually discover that I'm a connoisseur of bad dad jokes (that's redundant, come to think of it).

So, mix these all into a Venn Diagram and I could perhaps be defined as a Disney historian and writer, focusing on cats, dogs, and bad jokes. Close, but not quite. My avocation is writing about Disney historical figures, the "best in class" employees of The Walt Disney Company who have been named Disney Legends. Unfortunately, cats and dogs have not yet achieved this honor.

I've been writing about Disney Legends for Celebrations, beginning with Ub Iwerks which was featured in issue 25, published in late 2012.

Disney Legends covers the honorees I wrote for Celebrations issues between 2012 to 2016, spanning Celebrations issues 25 through 50. Volume 2 will cover honorees published 2017 and onward. It's in the works now. Each article has been lightly edited for clarity and to reflect any major timeline changes.

This was all possible when Tim Foster, founder of Celebrations, took a chance on an unknown writer. He published my first article in issue six, regarding "Dining on the Disney Cruise Line," back in 2009. I'm still a writer for the magazine, which recently published issue 82.

During the downtime of Covid, I used the opportunity to write my first Disney book. "Walt Goes to Washington: Finding Disney in DC" explores the intersections between Walt, the

Disney company and Washington DC, such as the Department of Defense, the Library of Congress, the Supreme Court, and the Smithsonian Institution, for example. You can find an order link on my website below.

For more information on Celebrations, visit https://celebrationspress.com.

And if you want to hear about Disney cats and dogs, among other Disney topics, and my occasional bad dad joke, tune in to the Celebrations bi-weekly podcast: https://celebrations-press.com/celebrations-disney-podcast/.

For more information about me, visit https://jamieheckerwriter.com and https://kmfphotography.com.

In the meantime, enjoy this collection of diverse Disney Legends.

Jamie Hecker
September 2023

# THE DISNEY LEGENDS PROGRAM

Legend. Greatest of all time. Hero. These are some of the many accolades bestowed on individuals for accomplishments in their field. Every major league in sports has its own hall of fame, signifying the best of the best in football, baseball, basketball, and hockey. For the military, the Medal of Honor is granted to those who have performed immeasurable acts of valor. For civilians, The Presidential Medal of Freedom is the highest honor available, for "an especially meritorious contribution to the security or national interests of the United States."

With this backdrop, it stands to reason that The Walt Disney Company, a century old in October 2023, has many men, women and children who have distinguished themselves in service to Disney. Since 1987, Disney has been honoring its own with the title of Disney Legend. As of September 2022, 304 recipients have been honored. The recipients come from all facets of the company – parks and resorts, Imagineering, animation, television, film, music, voicework, attractions and merchandising, to name a few. Honorees have also come from Disney partners such as ABC Television, Pixar, Marvel and Lucasfilm.

The Disney Legends program has a fascinating origin story. When the executive team of Michael Eisner and Frank Wells arrived in 1984, they brought with them a new energy for the Disney brand. Synergy was king, and to help promote the updated *The Shaggy Dog* film, its star Fred MacMurray was invited to Burbank to help celebrate the "shaggy dog" month. The occasion was that the film was recently colorized from its original black-and-white version and set for debut on the Disney Channel.

MacMurray was a seasoned actor and star in numerous Disney hits including *The Absent-Minded Professor, Son of Flubber, Follow Me Boys* and *The Happiest Millionaire.* Part of the celebration included having MacMurray perform a handprint-in-cement ceremony at the Burbank studio, like that of Hollywood stars in front of the Grauman Chinese Theater (now the TCL Chinese Theater). On October 10, 1987, MacMurray was honored as the first Disney Legend. Eisner didn't see it ending there, and the Legends program was deemed the official and henceforth, it would honor and celebrate legends of The Walt Disney Company.

No Legends were named in 1988, but in 1989 the program continued in grand fashion, inducting all of the Nine Old Men, Walt's most gifted character animators, and Ub Iwerks, Walt's critical animator in the early years, notably on the early Mickey Mouse shorts. A select committee, headed then by Roy E. Disney, reviewed candidates each year and selected a handful for induction. Roy Disney passed away in 2009, but the committee has continued his work since.

Disney Legends were honored yearly from 1989 to 2009, and then on a biennial basis, with the ceremony taking place at the D23 Expo, Disney's official fan club celebration. However, the expected 2021 D23 Expo was postponed a year due to the global Covid pandemic. The tradition of handprints in cement continued and with the growing number of recipients, it became clear that a formal site for the inductees was needed. In 1998, to help commemorate the 75th anniversary of The Walt Disney Company, the Legends Plaza was created. It resides on the northwest corner of the Burbank studio, in front of the Team Disney building, with its unique façade of the seven dwarfs serving as caryatids. The Legends Plaza has an open courtyard, with each side consisting of columns hosting handprint plaques of Legends, save for those honored posthumously. Within the courtyard are several notable statues – first there is the famous Walt Disney and Mickey Mouse looking outward, present at both Disneyland and The Magic Kingdom. Second is the tribute to Walt's brother Roy, featuring him sitting alongside Minnie Mouse on a park bench. Finally, there is a large-scale reproduction of the award presented to recipients. Its three essential features are, as formally stated by The Walt Disney Company, "The Spiral—(which) stands for imagination, the power of an idea. The Hand—(which) holds the gifts of skill, discipline and craftsmanship. The Wand and the Star—(which) represent magic: the spark that is ignited when imagination and skill combine to create a new dream."

The Legends induction has been used on several occasions for specific honorees. In 1997, the ceremony was held at Disneyland Paris to celebrate that park's fifth anniversary. All eighteen recipients were of European origin. This same technique was repeated five years later at Disneyland Paris for its tenth anniversary. Ten Legends, again of European origin, were inducted. Notable members of that class include director Robert Stevenson (*Mary Poppins*) and songwriter Phil Collins. Disneyland's golden jubilee was a year-long celebration in 2005, so naturally all the Disney Legends that year were affiliated with Walt Disney Parks and Resorts or Walt Disney Imagineering. In 2011, five singers who performed as animated princesses on film were collectively awarded the honor of being a Disney Legend and gave a rousing performance at the D23 Expo induction ceremony.

The Walt Disney Company and its parks, films and television offerings is an integral part of the American identity, and even has a broad, global outreach. It's only fitting that the company has so many talented men and women to honor. With the continued growth of The Walt Disney Company, there should be plenty of future Disney Legends to be honored in the future.

Walt and Roy Disney with their new star, Mickey Mouse, at the 2719 Hyperion Avenue studio. On November 18, 1932, at the fifth annual Academy Awards presentation, Walt was honored with an Academy Honorary Award Oscar for the creation of Mickey Mouse.

# HOW IT ALL BEGAN —
## THE STORY OF WALT AND ROY DISNEY BEFORE BURBANK

The Disney Legends program, established in 1987, is the highest honor The Walt Disney Company can bestow upon its employees. Numerous animators, film and television stars, and Imagineers, to name a handful of categories, have been inducted into Disney's highest order. However, two expected names aren't on the list - Walt Disney and Roy O. Disney. The two brothers, who founded the company in 1923, created an environment where their creative peers could excel. Walt and Roy's surname alone merits their inclusion as Legends.

Much is known of contemporary Disney company history, after the company moved into its spacious campus at Burbank. However, the early years of the company - from 1923 to 1940 - are equally important, and in many regards, more so. Had Walt and Roy failed with *Snow White and the Seven Dwarfs*, the first ever feature-length animation film, the young studio perhaps wouldn't have survived. Instead, the film was a financial and critical hit, and the brothers were able to take the company to the next level.

To borrow a phrase: how did it all begin? Walt and Roy, siblings together growing up and reunited as adults in Los Angeles, each followed different paths to the company. Roy, born in 1893, was eight years older than Walt, born in 1901. They formed a childhood bond during their formative years in idyllic Marceline, Missouri. After relocating to Kansas City, Roy struck out as a young adult and got a job as a bank clerk, in 1912. Several years later, he joined the Navy toward the end of World War I. Walt, too young to enlist, instead lied about his age and joined the American Ambulance Corps. He shipped overseas to support the troops, but the war was already over. Both men returned from Europe and took alternate paths. Walt began pursuing his animation dreams in Kansas City, but his Laugh-O-Gram Studio foundered and went into bankruptcy. Roy was recuperating in a Veterans Administration hospital in Los Angeles, where the dry climate was aiding his recovery from tuberculosis. Roy beckoned Walt to get a fresh start in Los Angeles, and in July 1923 Walt made the fateful train trip from Kansas City to Los Angeles.

Roy, now out of the hospital, and Walt stayed with their uncle Robert Disney on 4406 Kingswell Avenue in Los Angeles. After striking out in Hollywood where he sought directing duties, Walt returned to his love of animation. He rekindled a business relationship with Margaret Winkler to continue developing his hybrid animation and live-action series dubbed the Alice Comedies. On October 15th, Margaret sent Walt a contract for six Alice shorts. Walt pressed Roy to be his business partner and the next day they formally signed the contract. The Disney Brothers Cartoon Studio was born. Uncle Robert's standalone garage was pressed into service for studio space and is roundly considered the official genesis of the company. The garage, preserved from demolition, is on display at the Stanley Ranch Museum in nearby Garden Grove, California. The Disney brothers quickly needed more space, and the next studio location was a room for rent at a nearby realty office at 4651 Kingswell Avenue. By February 1924, with the Alice Comedies keeping the company afloat, they moved into larger office space next door, at 4651 Kingswell. The rent was $35 a month. This was the operating studio for nearly two years. In July of 1925, Walt and Roy put down a $400 deposit on an empty lot on 2719 Hyperion Avenue. The growing company needed more room to stretch and moved into the new studio in January 1926. At the same time, at Roy's insistence, the company name was changed: going forward, it was now the Walt Disney Studio. Roy, ever mindful that his brother was the creative mastermind of the company, gladly let Walt take center stage. Hyperion would remain the studio for the next fourteen years, and this is where the magic truly happened. With Roy's careful financial guidance and Walt's abundant creativity, the Walt Disney Studio, like Walt and Roy's passage from Marceline to Kansas City and on to Los Angeles, grew from adolescence into a fully mature company. At Hyperion, the company went from the Alice Comedies - 56 total - to fully animated shorts. Disney's first star, Oswald the Lucky Rabbit, hit the silver screen in July 1927. The Disney brothers were pioneers in the animation industry and they yielded many additional firsts, notably sound, color and animation training.

Following Oswald, Walt unveiled Mickey Mouse, now the icon of the company who made a spectacular debut, with synchronized sound no less, on November 18, 1928, in *Steamboat Willie*. So dedicated to the overall quality of his product that Walt reluctantly sold his prized roadster to help fund cost overruns associated with *Steamboat Willie*.

Disney animation evolved with the advent of the Silly Symphonies, a free-form style of animation where directors, animators and story artists could test and push boundaries. In this realm, the first color animation was released - *Flowers and Trees*, in July 1932. Disney maximized the benefits of a multiplane camera, first with its 1937 Academy Award-winning short *The Old Mill* and next with the seminal *Snow White and the Seven Dwarfs*.

Another first for Disney, monumental in both how it saved the company precious production funds and enhanced the story development process, was the use of storyboards. This series of quick sketches allowed writers to flesh out a story from beginning to end, identifying weaknesses to be resolved and inconsistencies to be fixed. Unlike live action, where editing is done after principal photography, an animated short or feature needs to be fully formed before ink and paint are applied, to reduce production cost overruns. Roy, in charge of the financial ledgers, no doubt cherished this innovation.

Animated features were becoming as much about works of art as engaging storytelling. To that end, Walt put his skilled animators through rigorous and formal art training, first by sending his men to the nearby Chouinard Art Institute for evening classes, and later by having Chouinard instructors set up shop directly at the Hyperion Studio. Walt and Roy were gradually elevating animation, from rudimentary cartoons to a more elegant art form, particularly human anatomy.

The Walt Disney Studio greatly matured during its fourteen years at Hyperion. The financial success of *Snow White* allowed Walt and Roy to build a new studio from scratch in Burbank. The patterns and habits that began at Hyperion amplified there, allowing the company to push through artistic and technical barriers, not only in animation but also eventually in live-action movies, television and theme parks.

The Disney brothers shared a common goal but went about it their own style. Walt was confident and flamboyant, while Roy was reserved and unassuming. A home movie filmed at the Hyperion Studio clearly puts both personalities on display. During an employee softball game, Walt displayed confidence and swagger when he was at bat. When the camera drifted over to Roy, he quietly stepped out of camera range, opting not to be in frame. This simple scene defined them and how they each, in their own way, built an iconic American brand.

From left to right: Back row: Milt Kahl, Marc Davis, Frank Thomas, Eric Larson, and Ollie Johnston. Front row: Woolie Reitherman, Les Clark, Ward Kimball, and John Lounsbery.

# WALT'S NINE OLD MEN —
## THE GIFTED DISNEY CHARACTER ANIMATORS

Disney fans and historians regularly hear the phrase Disney's Nine Old Men. What exactly does that mean, and who are they? Walt Disney Productions, in the post-war years, formed an internal review board to assess where efficiencies in the animation process could be made. animator Frank Thomas ascertained that during one of the board meetings in the early 1950s, Walt noted that it consisted of nine of his vaunted character animators, those who were tasked with creating silver screen icons such as Sleeping Beauty, Peter Pan, Tinker Bell, and Cruella de Vil. Walt publicly used the phrase 'nine old men,' in reference to the nine animators at the meeting. Alphabetically, they are: Les Clark, Marc Davis, Ollie Johnston, Milt Kahl, Ward Kimball, Eric Larson, John Lounsberry, Wolfgang Reitherman and Frank Thomas. Collectively, some or all of them have worked on Disney animated features ranging from *Snow White and the Seven Dwarfs* to *The Fox and the Hound*. Ironically, his animators were in the mid 30s to mid 40s when Walt dubbed them as 'old.' They may not necessarily be household names, but each artist left his mark on the Disney company's legacy. For example, Davis went from animation to WED Enterprises where he added humor to attraction classics such as The Jungle Cruise and Pirates of the Caribbean, Reitherman would eventually turn to directing animated features, and Johnston and Thomas collectively wrote *Disney Animation:*

*The Illusion of Life*, a tome that outlines the Disney style of character animation and is widely regarded by artists young and old as the authoritative guide to animation.

Five of the nine are featured in this book. Four in this chapter, and a fifth, Marc Davis, is featured in Chapter 12.

# WARD KIMBALL
## 1989

Walt Disney changed the field of film animation, gradually elevating it to an elegant art form. He provided the vision and direction, but countless animators, story supervisors and technicians, to name a few groups, brought the shorts and feature films to life. Walt even had his fabled Nine Old Men, a core group of animators who were the backbone of the company. Ward Kimball, an esteemed member of this group, often cut against the grain of animation conventions, but his style and contributions to Disney animation are legendary, ranging from subtle grace to outlandish caricatures.

Kimball, born in 1914 in Minneapolis, Minnesota, developed an early fascination with animation, notably the Sunday newspaper color comics, as well as performance art, especially the slapstick style of vaudeville. For a period of time, he lived with his grandparents, who encouraged his budding interest in art and animation. His family, which relocated often during his youth, eventually moved to California, and following high school, Kimball received a scholarship to the Santa Barbara School of Arts. Upon graduation, he found suitable employment as a graphic artist but seeing the Disney Silly Symphony classic *Three Little Pigs* on the big screen proved to be a turning point in his life. He was awestruck at what Disney was creating and wanted to be a part of it. He collected his best work samples and applied to Walt Disney Productions, and was immediately hired, in April 1934.

New hires at the company were given "in-between" assignments, fleshing out the animation lines that senior animators had already completed, and Kimball began his Disney work in this manner. His talents were soon noted by the more established senior animator Ham Luske, who took in Kimball as his protege. Recalled Kimball, "Ham gave me a lot of responsibility and that's the way you learn. . . . He told me you couldn't caricature until you can analyze, draw, and shot the real object, the real character."

Disney was working on its ambitious *Snow White and the Seven Dwarfs*, and Kimball diligently animated several scenes which were ultimately cut out of the final film. Dejected, he nearly left Disney until he was presented with a new challenge: create and animate a new character that would serve as a conscience to a wooden marionette boy who comes to life. Kimball created the timeless Jiminy Cricket for *Pinocchio* and served as the directing animator for him. Creating the appearance of Jiminy was no small task. Recalled Kimball, "I did twelve or fourteen versions and gradually cut off all the appendages. I ended up with a little man, really, wearing spats and a tail coat that suggested folded wings . . . The audience accepts him as a cricket because the other characters say he is."

Kimball contributed to *Fantasia*, notably the character Bacchus from the pastoral symphony sequence. His next animation challenge was a relatively minor character in the Disney universe: the poetry loving dragon that serves as the centerpiece for the 1941 live-action and animation mix *The Reluctant Dragon.* Over half of the movie is a scripted tour of the Disney studios in Burbank, and Kimball makes a cameo during a sequence set in the animation department. He continued his artistic prowess on *Dumbo*, animating the scene in which the crows find Dumbo and Timothy Q. Mouse up in a tree.

Disney created two "goodwill" films following Disney's visit to Latin America sponsored by The Office of the Coordinator of Inter-American Affairs, an executive branch established by President Roosevelt to encourage western hemisphere unification during World War II. Kimball created what is considered his finest animation work - the outrageous, chaotic, and high-energy musical sequence featuring Donald Duck, Jose Carioca and Panchito Pistoles in *The Three Caballeros*. It's a brilliantly choreographed sequence that flies in all directions at once. Kimball fondly recalled, "That's the only animation I ever did that I'm uncritical of. I look at the damn song I did and I laugh and I grin as hard as the day I did it."

Kimball next turned his animation pencil to the American folklore character of Pecos Bill for the 1948 release of *Melody Time*, creating a lovable caricature of the Western hero. Disney's next release was a return to the fairy tale genre, with the sweeping *Cinderella* and a return to animation realism, or the 'illusion of life.' The animals, however, had less restrictions and Kimball animated Lucifer the cat and the mice Gus and Jaq as charming caricatures of evil and good. Kimball's next animation highlight was the wild and wooly Unbirthday party scene from *Alice in Wonderland*, released in 1951, bringing to life the outlandish Mad Hatter and the March Hare in the party scene that practically defines absurd.

The Walt Disney Company was continuously evolving, from shorts to feature length and into the new medium of television. Kimball, too, was expanding his contributions, now serving as a director. He helmed the Academy Award-winning short subject film *Toot, Whistle, Plunk and Boom*. The story outlined the four fundamental musical instrument groups and how they evolved, from cavemen to the present day. Kimball utilized a more modern, limited animation style that featured flat dimensions and asymmetrical design and a uniquely un-Disney look. He found the opportunity to direct liberating: "I was so relieved to get away from animation. I knew how to do it. I wanted to have some say about the content."

Kimball's next directorial contribution was grander in scale - the three-part science series he created for the *Disneyland* television program. Frontierland had Davy Crockett, Adventureland had the True-Life Adventures, but Tomorrowland needed forward-looking content. Kimball recalled the scientific article he read in *Collier's* magazine about space exploration, penned by Dr. Wernher Von Braun, the former German turned American scientist who eventually became NASA's space exploration architect, and proposed that Disney collaborate with him on a television series. Kimball worked closely with Von Braun on the scripts for the three-part series and the results were "Man In Space," "Man and the Moon" and "Mars and Beyond." "Man In Space" succinctly tapped into the country's fascination with space exploration. It was so successful that President Eisenhower requested a copy of it for a private screening at the Pentagon, no doubt helping to accelerate the country's budding civilian space program. "Man in Space" aired in 1955; NASA's first space exploration program, Mercury, was established three years later, leading to sub-orbital and then orbital manned space flight in 1961 and 1962, respectively.

Kimball wasn't just a prolific animator and director. Like Walt, he was also a railroad enthusiast and had his own backyard train dubbed Grizzly Flats. In his honor, the Disneyland Railroad named engine No. 5 the *Ward Kimball*. He was also an accomplished trombonist and helped form the Firehouse Five Plus Two, a Dixieland jazz band of fellow Disney artists.

Ward's personal credo perhaps best sums up his life's work: "(D)evelop an all-consuming curiosity for things both exotic and living. Read, observe, analyze, and above all be flexible . . . Keep an open mind and have fun. Take it from me, it's worth it!" For his contributions to The Walt Disney Company, Ward Kimball was named a Disney Legend in 1989, along with his fellow Nine Old Men.

# ERIC LARSON

## 1989

The legacy of Disney animation rests largely on the backs of Walt's most prolific character animators collectively known as the Nine Old Men. Their combine artistic skills in drafting, storytelling and animating helped set the bar of quality for Disney feature animation, beginning with *Snow White and the Seven Dwarfs*, the instant classic released in 1937. Eric Larson, one of Walt's Nine Old Men, was key to the continued artistic growth and commercial success of Disney animation.

Larson was born in 1905 in Cleveland, Utah and later moved to Salt Lake City. He lived on a ranch during his formative years which led to his strong association and talent for capturing the essence of animal characters. He informally developed his artistic skills while pursuing a degree in journalism at the University of Utah. After college, he traveled throughout the American west and ultimately settled in the Los Angeles area. While pursuing a career in writing for radio he connected with a Disney writer for guidance. Serendipity intervened, and Larson's animation sketches that he had been casually developing won him a job at Disney in 1933 as an in-between animator.

Larson's easy-going personality and natural animation skills were quickly noted by the veteran animators, and he moved up in rank, working directly under the tutelage of Ham

Luske. Within four years, Larson was making his mark, helping with the multiple animal sequences in *Snow White*. On *Pinocchio*, Disney's next feature animation film, Larson brought to life the impish personality of Figaro the cat. Recalled Larson about the character, "A four-year old kid is quick to feel hurt if he doesn't get what he wants. He is probably going to put on a show for us, a tantrum. Take an animal, like Figaro, move him around as a kitten would move. You don't take any liberties with that kind of acting but now you inject into him a personality of this young kid who is used to having everything he wanted. This is where we would cross from realism to fantasy, in my opinion."

On *Fantasia*, Larson was principally involved in the Pastoral Symphony sequence featuring multiple Pegasus and Centaurs. On *Bambi*, Larson brought to life Thumper, the Great Stag, and Owl. Larson personally supervised a crew of thirty, allowing him the opportunity to display his management skills. Recalled fellow Nine Old Men animators Frank Thomas and Ollie Johnston, "On *Bambi* (Larson) had the largest crew of any of the top men and there was always someone in his room with a problem, often nothing to do with the production. Eric was always patiently listening, occasionally counseling, but somehow he was still one of the best footage men in the studio. And to top it all, he was able to get footage out of most of his crew."

Larson continued his animation career on *The Three Caballeros* (the Flying Gauchito segment), *Make Mine Music* (Sasha the bird), *The Adventures of Ichabod and Mr. Toad* (the title characters), *Melody Time* (Johnny Appleseed), *Song of the South* (Br'er Rabbit, Br'er Fox and Br'er Bear), and *Fun and Fancy Free* (Jiminy Cricket).

Disney animation returned to high form with the 1950 release of *Cinderella*. Larson gracefully animated the young heroine of this film, perhaps his strongest character animation effort of his career. The next feature was *Alice in Wonderland*, for which Larson animated the caterpillar and the vitriolic Queen of Hearts. Disney's next feature was the timeless *Peter Pan*, for which Larson was tasked with the scene of Peter Pan and the Darling children flying from London to Neverland. On this assignment, he and his crew used the best available technology to them - the multiplane camera. "We not only used (the) multiplane, we had to work the hell out of that camera . . . exaggerations, going away from you and coming at you," Recalled Larson. "Besides drawing that we put emphasis on it by using camera tilts. It was a very beautifully worked out thing mechanically. It really has a certain thrill to it."

In the twilight of his animation career, Larson brought to life the effervescent Peg in *Lady and the Tramp*, Pongo and Perdita in *One Hundred and One Dalmatians*, various farm animals in *Mary Poppins*, Mowgli and Bagheera in *The Jungle Book*, Roquefort and Scat Cat in *The Aristocats*, and finally Kanga and Roo in *The Many Adventures of Winnie the Pooh*. In the late 1970's and 1980's, he served as an animation consultant for Disney.

Larson's impressive body of animation work is enough to qualify him as a Disney Legend, but it's what he did late in his career that is perhaps longer lasting. In the early 1970's, he established a recruitment and training program to identify and cultivate a new generation of animators. The highlights of his work include: Burny Mattinson (*Robin Hood*), Randy Cartwright (the flying carpet in *Aladdin*, Belle from *Beauty and the Beast*), Glen Keane (Ariel from *The Little Mermaid*, Beast from *Beauty and the Beast*, Rapunzel from *Tangled*), Andreas Deja (Jafar from *Aladdin*), Brad Bird (*Ratatouille*, *The Incredibles*), Tim Burton (*The Nightmare Before Christmas*), the directing team of Ron Clements and John Musker (*The Little Mermaid*, *Moana*), and John Lasseter (co-founder of Pixar, director of *Toy Story* and *Cars*). Deja, a fellow Disney Legend, spoke highly of his mentor: "No one was more concerned with passing on the Disney (animation) legacy than Eric."

Throughout his career, Larson abided by his guiding principle for animation: "Make a positive statement. Don't be ambiguous in what you're saying. Make it strong and clear." This was evident in the wide body of work he did for feature animation. Larson formally retired in 1986 after a 52-year career at Disney. He passed away two years later. He was posthumously named a Disney Legend in 1989.

# WOOLIE REITHERMAN
## 1989

In October 2023, The Walt Disney Company will be celebrating a century of operations. The backbone of The Walt Disney Company is clearly hand drawn animation. Walt and his cadre of animators gradually raised the bar on the quality and art of animation. Mickey Mouse shorts and Silly Symphonies all paved the way for feature length animation. Walt relied on the talents of key animators he dubbed the Nine Old Men; each one has earned the distinction of being named a Disney Legend. One of the nine is Wolfgang Reitherman, a prolific animator and director.

Born in Munich, Germany in 1909, Reitherman and his family migrated to the United States just two years later and settled in Kansas City, Missouri. By coincidence, he lived just a few blocks away from Roy O. Disney. His passion growing up was aviation, and he longed to be involved in the aircraft industry. He obtained his private pilot's license and briefly worked as a draftsman for Douglas Aircraft. During the Great Depression, however, he was unable to reliably stay employed in the aviation field, so he enrolled at the Chouinard Art Institute to formally study watercolor painting. His work caught the attention of his peers who recommended he apply to the Disney Studio. Upon graduation from Chouinard in 1933, he applied to and was hired at Disney. Reitherman was initially skeptical of animation; he enjoyed the lush, vibrant colors of painting. He perceived animation as a rote drill that would quickly become boring. He quickly discovered it was exactly the opposite. He recalled his initial reaction to seeing animation come to life - "I just felt this was a twentieth century art form, probably the most unique of anything that had appeared on the art horizon for decades since perspective. I was just fascinated that you could move these things. You can't move a painting. And all of the sudden, on a white sheet of paper, you could make something move." Wolfgang, who more commonly went by the nicknames Wooly or Woolie, had found his calling.

Reitherman's artistic skills allowed him to quickly jump into character animation, bypassing the traditional in-studio apprentice system. His first official work was on the 1934 Silly Symphony short *Funny Little Bunnies.* Next up for Reitherman was *The Wise Little Hen,* notable for introducing the temperamental fowl Donald Duck. Over time, Reitherman would contribute to over two dozen shorts, both as standalone pieces and package film entries. His contributions include notable entries such as *Hawaiian Holiday, Clock Cleaners, The Wind in the Willows* and *The Adventures of Ichabod and Mr. Toad.*

Following the steady success of the Silly Symphonies, Walt felt it was time to embark on a feature length animated movie - S*now White and the Seven Dwarfs*. Reitherman had the arduous task of animating the magic mirror, the Queen's mystic who is compelled to answer her questions. Reitherman devised a clever approach to minimally animating the face; he folded his paper in half and animated half the face, then traced it over to the other half to complete the symmetric facial animation. The result was an eloquently understated character that coldly conveyed his emotions. Reitherman fondly recalled the work he and his colleagues spent creating the film. "There was a great feeling of excitement in those days. We were actually poking into the unknown."

Reitherman continued with feature animation by working on oversized characters that featured intense action. In 1940's *Pinocchio*, he deftly brought to life Monstro the whale, keeping audiences on the edge of the seat with Pinocchio and Stromboli's harrowing escape from the beast. For a follow up, Reitherman animated the dramatic dinosaur fight scene in *Fantasia*. He successfully tackled other intense, larger-than-life characters including the Headless Horseman from *The Legend of Sleepy Hollow*, the crocodile from *Peter Pan* and Maleficent the dragon from *Sleeping Beauty*.

Over the span of his Disney career, Reitherman became close to the classic Disney character Goofy. He animated his outlandish antics in numerous shorts and package films, including the El Gaucho sequence from *Saludos Amigos*, *Goofy Gymnastics* and Goofy as an 'everyman' in various "How To" shorts such as *How to Ride a Horse, How to Fish* and *How to Swim.* Reitherman brought Goofy to life in a fashion that rivals Mickey Mouse and Donald Duck for Disney character icon status.

As his skill with the pencil and clout within feature animation grew, Reitherman furthered his contributions to Disney when he took on directorial duties. He helmed all feature animation films from 1963 to 1977, which included *The Sword in The Stone, The Jungle Book,* and *The Rescuers.* Following Walt's death in 1966, Reitherman performed the admirable task of keeping feature animation shored up. Fellow Disney Legend Frank Thomas recalled that Reitherman was a "very strong leader" during that trying period. His last film involvement for Disney was 1981's *Fox and the Hound,* for which Reitherman served as Co-Producer.

If Goofy represents Reitherman's wild side, then Winnie the Pooh sweetly reflects his overall skills as animator, director, and master of the short medium. He directed *Winnie the Pooh and the Honey Tree* (1966), *Winnie the Pooh and the Blustery Day* (1968), and *The Many Adventures of Winnie The Pooh* (1977), all treasured classics still to this day. Reitherman even added another Oscar to the Disney family when he won an Academy Award for Best Animated Short Film for *Blustery Day.*

Woolie Reitherman enjoyed a career at Disney that spanned six decades, from the mid 30's to the early 80's. He also found small but important roles for his three sons for voiceover work; Bruce Reitherman performed as Mowgli in *The Jungle Book* and the first iteration of Christopher Robin, and sons Richard and Robert each have voice credit for Wart, the young protagonist from *The Sword in the Stone.*

Reitherman retired from Disney after *The Fox and The Hound,* with a tremendous body of animation work to his credit. To borrow the phrase, when you do what you love, you'll never work a day in your life. He observed, "(animation) was a romance from the start. The minute you know you can make a drawing move, the static drawing loses its appeal; movement is life."

Reitherman tragically died in an automobile accident near his home in 1985. He was posthumously named a Disney Legend in 1989.

# FRANK THOMAS
## 1989

The legacy of The Walt Disney Company is entertainment, and its foundation is animation. From the rudimentary Alice Comedies, then Oswald the Lucky Rabbit, Mickey Mouse and next the Silly Symphonies series, Disney was gradually elevating animation to an elegant art form, culminating with the release ground-breaking *Snow White and the Seven Dwarfs*. Animating these characters was a daunting task since they had to be believable and genuine for an audience to relate. A young animator by the name of Frank Thomas served as one of eight animators assigned to the dwarfs, and he was tasked with creating a pivotal scene in the film, in which the dwarfs are tenderly crying over what they believe to be the dead body of snow white. The scene required deep emotional maturity, and Thomas, just twenty-four years old at the time, handled it perfectly. He was an actor who emoted with his pencil rather than body and voice. His forty-three-year career at Disney is defined by iconic characters and scenes, such as Bambi, Pinocchio, Captain Hook, Baloo and the romantic spaghetti dinner from *Lady And The Tramp*.

Frank Thomas was born in Santa Monica California in 1912. He attended Stanford University studying the Arts. While there, he met Ollie Johnson, who would also become a Disney animator and a life-long friend and colleague. After graduation, Thomas continued his education at the

Chouinard Art Institute in Los Angeles. In 1934, he applied for and was accepted to Disney as an "in-betweener," Disney's entry-level animating position. Fred Moore, the early Disney animator legend, took Thomas under his wings. Thomas' first significant animation work was the Mickey Mouse short *Mickey's Elephant*. He quickly rose in ranks and was part of the select crew working on Snow White. Thomas recalled the early brain-storming story sessions directed by Walt and how it helped the film. "One of the wildest things we ever did was started off so sane and simple. We were all going to talk about the characters: how they were going to walk, how they would move, how they would do all these different things. Walt would say, 'now this time you be Grumpy, you be Sleepy, you be so and so and let's see what we get here.'...it was about research, thinking about it and criticizing each other. 'I don't think Sleepy would do this, he's too sloppy.' The thing got funnier and funnier. But the thinking we went through was the valuable part...it was a new idea, something to try."

Thomas' next assignment was on *Pinocchio*. He, along with Johnson and Moore collaborated with Milt Kahl and Ham Luske to create the shape and form of the title character. Thomas and Kahl share credit for animating the puppet boy. Thomas' works shines brightly on the "I've got not strings" dance sequence. His next assignment was the long-developing *Bambi*. It was intended to be the follow-up to *Snow White*, but Disney realized that he needed time to refine the animation techniques needed for wildlife. Development started in 1939 but the movie wasn't released until 1942 when America was caught up in World War II.

Thomas and Kahl were assigned the young Bambi and had the clout to develop scenes without Walt's early supervision. Said Thomas, "When Milt and I started on *Bambi*, before the war, (Walt) told us, 'you know, don't show me anything until you're satisfied with it.' It was over two months' time that Walt waited. I did the art where baby Bambi runs up the hill and the butterfly lights on his tail and he's just learned to say, 'bird' and Thumper says, 'that's not a bird, it's a butterfly." Upon showing their work to Walt, Thomas received rare praise from him. "(Walt) had tears in his eyes and he said, 'fellas, this is pure gold.' That was one of my prize moments of all time. He never did it again."

With feature animation now taking center stage, the studio was honing and refining its talent. A core group of nine animators — dubbed the Nine Old Men, a nod to the phrase coined for the Supreme Court during the Roosevelt presidency — served as principal and directing animators for all feature length films. Thomas proudly served as a member of this elite group of Disney artisans.

Thomas had the good fortune to Join Walt and other Disney personnel on the South America goodwill tour in 1941. Thomas witnessed a different side of Walt, outside of the studio culture. While on the tour, Thomas recalled, "Walt would say, 'we've all been working pretty hard, so next Tuesday we're going to take the day off and we're going to rest.' We'd start out resting at 7:00 in the morning. 'We'll have a football game on the beach.' It was the most exhausting day he had. But he rested the way he worked." An interesting sidebar to this trip is that Frank's son Ted captured the spirit of it in his documentary, *Walt and El Grupo*.

Thomas continued his stellar animation career with notable characters, even some of Disney's most famous villains. His Captain Hook has the right blend of sinisterness and bluster. He animated the evil Stepmother from *Cinderella*, imbuing her with a cold and calculated personality. In *The Jungle Book*, he handled Baloo the bear, and recalled the challenge of the scene following the return of the 'man cub' Mowgli to his village. As the heartbroken bear leaves, said Thomas, "there should be an aimless feeling to Baloo's walk, in contrast to his normal expansive confident manner."

Perhaps the best-known image from Thomas' animation career is the tender scene between the elegant Lady and the street-savvy Tramp who enjoy a romantic spaghetti and meatball dinner while being serenaded, which climactically ends with a tender kiss as a single strand of spaghetti is shared. Although the stars are canines, Thomas perfectly captured the spirit of new romance that transcends us all, allowing filmgoers of all ages to connect with it.

Not only was Thomas a top-rate animator but he was also an amazing pianist, performing with the in-house jazz band Firehouse Five Plus Two. Other notable Disney veterans such as Ward Kimball and Harper Goff were in the rollicking quintet. What started out as a hobby band soon developed into a nationally famous band which performed frequently at Disneyland and released over a dozen albums.

Thomas' Disney career ended with his retirement in 1978 after nearly twenty feature animation films to his credit. His time at Disney spanned many changes, from the early studio on Hyperion to the spacious Burbank facility that included an extensive backlot for the company's venture into live-action television and films. Thomas spoke glowingly of Walt: "He was the best director we had as far as knowing how to handle people, knowing how to get the work out of them. Walt had the ability to make you work over your head."

Thomas, along with his Disney colleague and close friend Ollie Johnson remain linked even in retirement. Together, they authored the seminal work on animation, *Disney Animation: The Illusion of Life*. This 500 plus page masterpiece is considered the authoritative work on film animation.

For his lifelong contributions to The Walt Disney Company, Frank Thomas was named a Disney Legend in 1989.

# BRINGING DONALD DUCK TO LIFE

Clockwise from upper left: Jack Hannah (with Clarence "Ducky" Nash posing with a Donald Duck story board), Carl Barks, Al Taliaferro, and Clarence "Ducky" Nash

The legacy of The Walt Disney Company is built upon animation, featuring characters with genuine personalities. Mickey Mouse, of course, is an American original and the iconic image of the company. There's a reason the phrase "it was all started by a mouse" resonates so well. But Mickey isn't the only endearing character from the early years of the company. Six years after *Steamboat Willie*, Walt introduced a new character that equally fascinates and entertains - Donald Duck. He made his debut in the 1934 Silly Symphony short *The Wise Little Hen*, and was an instant hit, with his dual character traits of joyful exuberance and a thinly controlled hot temper. His unique voice, a mix of garbled quackery and semi-intelligible words, also helped him rise in fame. Donald Duck was the perfect vehicle for exploring new character dynamics; Mickey was increasingly becoming the ambassador of the company and had less latitude for wild adventures, so Donald took on that mantle. In fact, Donald Duck is so popular he eclipses Mickey in screen time in Disney shorts and animated features, and in Disney comics. He's equally present at the theme parks and Disney Cruise Line ships. With his broad appeal and legacy, it's no surprise to learn that a talented group of men share a collective responsibility for Donald Duck's fame.

Jack Hannah (1992) is largely responsible for the success of the Donald Duck cartoon shorts that proliferated from the 1930's to the 1960's. Hannah's Disney career began in 1933. Like most animators at the studio, he began as an in-between and cleanup artist on Donald Duck and Silly Symphony shorts, but quickly rose through the ranks. In 1939 he transitioned to the story department and used his wild imagination to create tales for the short-tempered fowl. A few years later, Hannah was again promoted, this time to director. It's here that he applied his masterful touch to over eighty shorts, many of which featured Donald Duck. Eight times he was nominated for an Academy Award. Hannah even ventured into the new medium of television, directing many episodes of Walt Disney's Wonderful World of Color. Disney was no stranger to the mixture of live-action and animation, and the animated Donald made numerous appearances on the television show interacting with Walt at the studio. Hannah, whose Disney career was deeply connected with Donald Duck, recalled a peculiar story about the star. To help pay off a bar tab and earn some extra cash, he painted a mural of three Donald Duck bowling poses inside a San Diego bar. "I got permission from Roy O. Disney," Hannah recalled. "I didn't dare go to Walt!"

Hannah's work with Donald also extended into print, working with Carl Barks (1991) to develop comic books that featured the feathered fowl. In 1942, *Donald Duck Finds Pirate Gold* debuted to the public. Barks continued to work on Donald Duck comics for the next twenty-five years until his retirement. Barks, like Hannah, joined The Walt Disney Company in the 1930's and began in animation. He too rose in ranks to the story department and worked on over thirty Donald Duck shorts. Barks is also credited with expanding the universe of Donald Duck, first by introducing Huey, Dewey and Louie in the comic books and then the 1938 animated short *Donald's Nephews*. Barks next introduced Donald's wealthy uncle Scrooge McDuck in 1947 in the comics. Barks developed the metropolis of Duckburg for the comics, and Barks' legacy and body of work led to the popular animated television series *Duck Tales*. The early Donald Duck comic books are a valuable commodity, which led Barks, at his Disney Legends ceremony, to wryly observe: "I want to thank all the kids that bought my comic books for a dime and are now selling them for $2,000."

Comic books weren't the only venue for Donald Duck. Comic strips are a syndicated staple of daily and weekly newspapers and in the 1930's, Disney only granted Mickey Mouse this exclusive access. Disney ventured further with comic strips with the introduction of the Silly Symphony Sunday comic strip series. In 1935, a year after his animation debut, Donald Duck appeared periodically in the Silly Symphony strip. Al Taliaferro (2003), a Disney animator who began his career working on the Mickey Mouse comic strip, was responsible for Donald's work in the Silly Symphony strip. But Al had bigger ideas for the duck, believing that he could star outright in his own comic strip. Taliaferro, described by fellow comic strip animator Floyd Gottfredson as an "ambitious guy," pitched his idea to management but was initially rebuffed. Walt's brother Roy oversaw the comic strip division and didn't initially share the same vision as Taliaferro. Al even went to the top with his idea. "I ran into Walt in the hall one day and told him I thought it would be a good idea to do another strip using Donald Duck. Walt had a habit of raising his eyebrow and you'd know you'd hit a chord somewhere," Taliaferro would recall. To make his case, Taliaferro drew three weeks' worth of strips and eventually won Roy over. The Donald Duck strip debuted on February 7, 1938, drawn and inked by Taliaferro, and was an instant hit with the public.

Donald Duck is perhaps most famous for his irascible personality, often flying into an incoherent rage. His unique voice mannerisms are a core part of his personality. His spoken words are mixed with quackery gibberish and when perturbed, his rants are unintelligible but highly memorable. Clarence "Ducky" Nash (1993) has the honor of being the original voice of Donald. He parlayed his childhood habit of mimicking barnyard animals into a fifty-year career at Disney. Nash was in Los Angeles performing in radio shows doing animal impressions. In 1933, he paid a visit to the Disney studios to pitch his vocal services, aware they were regularly animating animals. Nash auditioned his billy goat voice and made a fabulous first impression. Walt heard the audition and immediately stated "That's our duck." Nash made his Disney debut in 1934 and continued to voice Donald through 1983's *Mickey's Christmas Carol* and appeared at numerous occasions celebrating Donald's fiftieth birthday. Not only did Nash provide the voice of Donald in all animated form, but he also provided the Scottish brogue of Scrooge McDuck. He even took the extraordinary step of dubbing Donald's voice in different languages, learning to quack in French, Chinese and German.

For their collective work on Donald Duck, Hannah, Barks, Taliaferro and Nash have all been named Disney Legends.

# The Imagineers

Walt Disney continuously dreamed of a theme park to showcase the various Disney intellectual properties. The earliest idea was a Mickey Mouse Park that would be adjacent to the Burbank studio, but that idea quickly outgrew the limited real estate available. Walt pressed on, despite concern from brother Roy, about identifying suitable property and how to create his wondrous playland. The conclusion to that move was the opening of Disneyland on July 17, 1955. But how does a company with no history of theme parks design one? Rather than outsource the project, Walt leaned on his talented employees at his company, ranging from animators, story artists and machine shop mechanics to blend their know-how. For purposes of keeping the design group separate from Walt Disney Productions, a publicly held company with a Board of Directors, Walt created his own private company named WED Enterprises on December 16, 1952. WED, of course, is the initials of Walter Elias Disney.

WED employees were tasked with the design of the park and attractions. The situation was unique, given that Walt's private company was doing work for Walt Disney Productions. To keep shareholders appeased, in March 1953 the Board of Directors of Walt Disney Productions agreed to license Walt Disney's name for forty years, give Walt Disney a personal services contract for seven years for $3,000 per week and 5-10 percent of what the company collects from the use of Walt's name on anything outside of production. WED Enterprises would design and build attractions for Disneyland and sell them to Walt Disney Productions at cost plus overhead.

WED would continue its work with additions to Disneyland, including the groundbreaking use of Audio-Animatronic characters. WED continued its work on the Walt Disney World parks and resorts, the overseas parks, and ships for the Disney Cruise Line, to showcase its highlights.

WED Enterprises was merged into Walt Disney Productions in 1964, and on February 3, 1986, WED Enterprises was rebranded as Walt Disney Imagineering (WDI), a name that reflects the core tasks of its employees – imagination and engineering.

# X ATENCIO
## 1996

At Epcot, Walt Disney World's most ambitious theme park, guests can witness the grand span of human communication when they experience Spaceship Earth, the park's distinctive and iconic 180-foot-tall geodesic sphere. One of the pivotal scenes in the attraction reviews the Renaissance, where Europe emerged enlightened from the Middle Ages. Artists such as Michelangelo, who were versatile in multiple skills, led to the phrase 'Renaissance Man.' Many men and women inside and out of Walt Disney Imagineering contributed to Spaceship Earth's various iterations, including Francis Xavier Atencio. Given the wide scope of contributions he has made to The Walt Disney Company, it seems fitting to consider him a Renaissance Man. Atencio worked for Disney as an animator, story writer, stop-motion animator, and lyricist, to name a few.

Atencio, who has personally and professionally gone by the shortened moniker "X" given to him by childhood peers, was born on September 4,1919 in Walsenburg, Colorado. With natural artistic talents, he gravitated toward the famous Chouinard Art Institute in Los Angeles, long affiliated with Disney for producing top-line animation talent. Atencio spent just one semester at Chouinard before he, at the suggestion of his instructors, submitted his portfolio to Disney. In 1938, Atencio was hired as an apprentice animator and earned the grand sum of $12 a week. It was an ideal time to be a Disney animator, following the break-through *Snow White and the Seven Dwarfs*. Atencio's early work was on *Pinocchio, Dumbo* and *Fantasia*. His animation career was put on hold while he served his country during World War Two in the United States Army Air Corps, as a photo intelligence officer.

Following the war, Atencio returned to Disney where he resumed his animation career. He widened his skills by developing story experience on the original *Mickey Mouse Club* television show. Atencio delved next into the filmmaking side of the Disney company. He formed an artistic partnership with Bill Justice by creating stop-motion animation shorts and sequences for feature films, including the title piece for *The Parent Trap* and the nursery cleanup scene from *Mary Poppins*. Atencio, however, ultimately found the work too tedious and admitted he didn't have the patience for it.

In 1965, Walt Disney himself transferred Atencio to WED Industries, the precursor to today's Walt Disney Imagineering. His first assignment involved the Primeval World diorama on the Disneyland Railroad. It involved retooling the dinosaur scene from WED's attraction Ford Magic Skyway, created for the 1964 New York World's Fair.

It was Atencio's next project that left an indelible mark on both himself and the Disney company. Walt called upon X to create the script for the long gestating attraction Pirates of the Caribbean. Atencio's initial reaction was, "I had never done any scripting before, but Walt seemed to know that's what I could do." Not only did Atencio craft the snappy dialog that guests have been enjoying for over four decades, but he also wrote the jaunty lyrics to "Yo Ho (A Pirate's Life For Me)." Recalled Atencio, "I did . . . the auctioneer scene and sent it over to (Walt). He said, 'that's fine, keep going.' And then after the script was done, I said 'I think we should have a little song in there.' I had an idea for a lyric and a melody. I recited it to Walt. I thought he'd probably say, 'that's great, get the Sherman Brothers to do it.' Instead, he said, 'that's great, get George Bruns to do the music.' So that's how I became a songwriter."

*Yo ho, yo ho, a pirate's life for me.*
*We pillage, we plunder, we rifle and loot*
*Drink up me 'earties, yo ho.*
*We kidnap and ravage and don't give a hoot.*
*Drink up me 'earties, yo ho.*

Atencio's jolly lyrics have withstood the test of time and are now part and parcel of Disney's Pirates of the Caribbean mythology. His contributions to the attraction did not end with the hearty pirate tale. Atencio also provided the voice of the talking pirate skull who admonishes guests with this grim warning: "Ye come seekin' adventure with salty old pirates, eh? Sure, you've come to the proper place."

With the rousing success of Pirates on his resume, Atencio was tasked by Marty Sklar and Richard Irvine to develop a script for the Haunted Mansion, another WED project with a long development cycle. Claude Coats and Marc Davis had worked out the major design elements, contrasting the spooky with the playful. For Atencio, his assignment was to write the show dialog. "This was just straight narration. I had to try and get in in a kind of spooky frame of mind, but not too spooky." Atencio also wrote the lyrics for the Haunted Mansion's signature song, "Grim Grinning Ghosts." Atencio also provided the attraction's whimsical sendoff at the end with the various hitch-hiking ghosts that board each Doom Buggy, which he confesses was initially an afterthought. It was a gimmick, he reflected, that worked great.

Atencio's career with WED continued at Disneyland with his work on Adventure Thru Inner Space. He contributed to Walt Disney World at the former Magic Kingdom attraction If You Had Wings. At EPCOT Center, he made his mark with contributions to Spaceship Earth, World of Motion and the Mexico Pavilion.

Atencio retired from The Walt Disney Company in 1984 but continued to work as a consultant to Walt Disney Imagineering before his death in 2017. In 1996, for his wide body of Disney work, Francis "X" Xavier Atencio was named a Disney Legend.

Upon reflection of his four decades of service to The Walt Disney Company as both an artist and an Imagineer, Atencio is most proud of his work for WED. "In my case of being a writer, I fell into it. It's a talent I didn't realize I had in myself. Walt put the finger on me and said go and do it. I went and did it and it was one of the greatest things that ever happened to me."

# BLAINE GIBSON

**1993**

Blaine Gibson, a name familiar with many Disney fans, was named a Disney Legend in 1993 to honor his lifetime work for The Walt Disney Company. From 1939 to 1983, his contributions included feature film animation, and his passion for sculpting led to his involvement with Walt Disney Imagineering, where he created sculptures that were used as the basis for President Lincoln in Great Moments with Mr. Lincoln at the 1964 New York World's Fair. His sculpting further contributed to the Audio-Animatronic characters in The Pirates of the Caribbean and The Hall of Presidents attractions. After retirement, he returned to the Disney Company to create his crowning achievement, the Partners statue at both Disneyland and the Magic Kingdom in Walt Disney World.

Gibson, who hails from Rocky Ford, Colorado, wasn't formally trained in the arts but had an instinct for shape and form and a keen sketching ability. He was enrolled at Colorado University but hadn't yet taken any formal art classes. The Walt Disney Company was flying high on the heels of the smashing success of *Snow White and the Seven Dwarfs*, and in early 1939, Gibson's mother suggested he send some of his sketches to Disney. The Disney animation application included strict instructions. Recalled Blaine, "specifically it has to be on regular typing paper. It has to be in HB lead pencil, and it cannot be shaded, it has to be just line. Well, when you're doing animation, the linear work is how they can tell whether you can (line) draw. When you start shading in, that kind of fakes it. When you can draw you can do things that look like they're in three dimension without it being shaded. So I tried to comply as closely as I could to all of their orders." Gibson's work impressed Disney animators and he was hired in the spring of 1939.

He rose in ranks in the animation department, beginning as an in-between artist and assistant animator. His list of credits eventually included *Fantasia, Bambi, Alice in Wonderland* and *Peter Pan.* Gibson was quite content with being an animator for Disney, and he sought to establish himself as one of the premier artists at the Studio. However, it was his youthful passion that redirected his Disney career. In addition to animation, Gibson had a lifelong interest and talent for sculpting. As a boy in Colorado, his first sculptures were made from the mud and clay from the family farm's irrigation ditches, material that he fondly recalled as having the perfect consistency. While in California, he took evening classes in sculpture, honing and refining his technique. He would display his creations at work, and Walt became fascinated with them, seeing grand potential. At Walt's personal request, Gibson was transferred to WED Industries, the precursor to today's Walt Disney Imagineering. "I didn't think it was that important (of a job), but then I was told Walt was expecting me to work on these (sculpting) projects. So I said to myself, 'what the heck' and went to WED. I was never sorry after that."

Disneyland was in the early stages of development, and Walt foresaw sculptures and figures as a natural path to transition from the realm of two-dimensional films into a three-dimensional park. Gibson recalled Walt's early fascination with his modeling projects for the park. "Walt used to come in all the time, sit down, and say, 'What are you up to, Blaine?' He was always interested in everything we did. That's what impressed the most about him, his enthusiasm."

His early sculptures for Disneyland included the devils from Mr. Toad's Wild Ride and native Americans in the now extinct Indian Village in Frontierland, and the mermaids for the original Submarine Voyage. He also created small-scale sculptures called maquettes, upon which larger characters would be created, as seen on the pneumatically driven Jungle Cruise animals.

He remained as an animator for Disney and a sculptor for WED, but fully transitioned to Imagineering in 1961 when he was tasked with leading the sculpture department of WED's Design and Development Division. His rise in ranks matched Walt's ambition for pushing the boundaries of entertainment. WED was involved in several attractions for the 1964 New York

World's Fair. For the State of Illinois, WED developed a life-size Audio-Animatronic version of Abraham Lincoln. Gibson was tasked with sculpting the face of the sixteenth president which would serve as a model for the first human AA. To ensure as much authenticity as possible, Gibson used a "life mask" the President had done in 1860. Disney's Lincoln was made from mechanical parts, but his face was created from silicone rubber based on the sculpted bust.

Gibson's work with Mr. Lincoln and his natural ability as a sculptor led him to be a key player in the creation of the Hall of Presidents at Walt Disney World. An opening day attraction in October 1971, this classic show has entertained guests with its likeness of all our presidents. Gibson has personally sculpted every face prior to President Obama and his predecessors. Gibson retired from Disney in 1983, but returned for occasional work, such as adding the likeness of President Clinton and both Bushes to the Hall of Presidents, helping to update the attraction when a new Commander in Chief is inaugurated.

Gibson played an instrumental role in two other classic attractions in both Anaheim and Orlando. The Pirates of the Caribbean and the Haunted Mansion feature dozens of AA's and ghoulish images, which originated first as sketches by renowned Disney artists such as Marc Davis. From these sketches, Gibson would develop maquettes to work out the dimensions before full-sized products were created. From the finished sculptures, typically in modeling clay, AA figures would be created. After Gibson provided the finished face sculpture, other Imagineers would fabricate the AA based off the bust. Clothing hides the inner mechanical workings of the devices, but it's the expressive face and body movements that give them life.

Guests in the Haunted Mansion gleefully admire Gibson's signature work on the attraction, the hitchhiking ghosts, which were originally created as sculptures. Davis' sketches for Pirates played strongly on instantly recognizable humor, and Gibson sought to expand on that, creating caricatures of pirates that still retained a sense of honesty. Gibson recalled Walt's guidance for the pirates was to "keep them believable." This neatly tied into Gibson's guiding principle with all his work: "what we had to shoot for is the feeling that the sculpture could be alive. Sure, sculptures can be animated mechanically, but if they already have a spark of life inherent in their creation, they work a lot better in getting the viewer involved."

The pinnacle of Blaine's Disney career was a special commemoration for Walt and Mickey Mouse that allowed Gibson to create his most hallowed creation, the Partners statue, in the hub of both Disneyland and the Magic Kingdom.

Gibson was given the assignment of creating a statue of Walt Disney, to permanently honor him in the parks he created. The statue features a simple pose of Walt and Mickey Mouse holding hands, beaming at the park guests. Said Gibson, "I chose to depict Walt as he was in 1954. I think that was when Walt was in his prime. It was tough trying to match the media image of Walt Disney, the one the public knows, to the real Walt, the one we knew." The Partners statue was unveiled at Disneyland in 1993, the same year Blaine Gibson was bestowed with the Disney Legends honor.

Two years later, an identical Partners statue was placed at the hub of the Magic Kingdom in Walt Disney World. When asked about his creation, Gibson reflected that Walt was pointing down Main Street and saying to Mickey at his side, "Look at all the happy people who have come to visit us today."

# WATHEL ROGERS
## 1995

December 16, 1952, is a hallowed date in Disney history. It doesn't mark the release of an animated cinematic masterpiece, nor is it the date of an adventurous live-action film. The date marks the founding of WED Industries, Walt Disney's personal company that he created to develop Disneyland, a theme park unlike any other. Walt hand-picked his first generation of Imagineers, mostly artists from the animation studio, and gave them a daunting task - create a unique theme park and populate it with immersive and ground-breaking attractions. They had no blueprint to follow. They opened Disneyland in 1955 and designed its major updates such as Tomorrowland in 1959 and New Orleans Square in 1966. The natural progression of Imagineering technology eventually led to the development and refinement of Audio-Animatronics (AA's) for Disneyland, which was a natural evolution of the work the Disney company was doing. Walt himself said, "It's just another dimension on the animation we have been doing all our life." Many Disney Imagineers were involved in this new technology, but one stands out among the others - Wathel Rogers, dubbed "Mr. Audio-Animatronics."

Rogers was born in Stratton, Colorado in 1919. As a boy, he had a natural curiosity about mechanical toys, and found he was able to easily create unique devices out of whatever odds and ends he found available. He also had an innate artistic ability and found himself drawn to the Disney Company in 1937. He enhanced his skills at the Chouinard Art Institute (which would later become the California Institute of the Arts, under the tutelage of Walt Disney). Rogers enjoyed a successful early career at Disney, before and after his service in World War II. His screen credits include *Cinderella*, *Alice in Wonderland* and *Sleeping Beauty*. However, it was his youthful passion of mechanical tinkering that opened the door to his true calling with Disney. Walt came across model railroads Wathel had constructed and noted this unique skillset of his animator. This expertise was soon put to the test.

In 1951, Walt returned from one of his many trips with a small mechanical wind-up bird in a cage that would chirp and flutter. Walt asked Wathel to determine how the bird mechanically worked. He reverse-engineered it and discovered inside a tiny bellow and delicate cams that operated the avian. From such a small object came the inspiration for Audio-Animatronics. On the strength of his work with the bird, Rogers was tasked, along with Roger Broggie Sr., with creating a more sophisticated mechanical figure. Dubbed Project Little Man, it involved filming actor Buddy Ebsen against a grid backdrop as he performed a vaudeville dance. The machine shop then created a nine-inch-tall figure (1/8th scale to Ebsen) that danced via a complex set of cams, rods and pneumatic tubes. The first AA prototype was born. One critical observation, however, was that the external complexity of the cams and rods prohibited making a full-sized human AA. That technology would need time to develop and mature.

In this same timeframe, Rogers' mechanical expertise was coming into focus as well. He and Ub Iwerks were creating new devices and techniques for filming, such as camera cranes and rear-screen special effects. Wathel's career went from the animation table to the studio machine shop and eventually to WED in the same capacity. His early work included the breakthrough Circarama motion-picture concept, which featured a 360-degree film. His involvement with AA's continued in Disneyland on the various wildlife found along the Mine Train Through Nature's Wonderland update in 1960.

The Enchanted Tiki Room was the next major evolution in AA's. Opened in 1963, it's a whimsical musical show set in the lush tropics of the South Seas and features over 150 talking and singing birds. The AA technology matured significantly to allow pneumatic tubes and solenoids (electrical magnets) to operate within the birds. In its simplest terms, the programming was binary – on or off. A bird beak would be either open or closed. An eyelid would blink down or be open. A head turn would be either left or right. On the vast stage, the collective bird show was an impressive sight. However, the technology needed improvement before taking on a more ambitious subject - the human body.

Disney was ramping up efforts for the 1964 New York World's Fair, which for the first time would feature full size human AA's. Disney's passion for American history led to the development of Abraham Lincoln for the State of Illinois pavilion, and the Carousel of Progress would feature a typical American family at different junctions in history. Two significant developments in AA technology allowed these ambitious projects to proceed. Hydraulic lines were incorporated into the body figures to allow for complex movement that air pressure couldn't handle, and an analog programming technique was added for more fluid human movement. In simpler terms, the voltage could be regulated to allow for cleaner motion. Lincoln was a complex creation. Rogers created the AA with sixteen air lines for the head, ten to the hands and wrists, and fourteen hydraulic lines to control the body. Rogers' work continued to the AA's exterior as well. He observed that latex didn't properly mimic human skin and instead went with a rubber-like product called Duraflex, which "has a consistency much like human skin," he said. "It flexes as well as compresses. Rubber, for example, will flex, but won't compress correctly for our needs."

Rogers' work on human AA's didn't end with construction. He was also a key figure in programming the movement, essentially animating them. Disney made use of declassified government technology dubbed Waldo which could be used to design the movements. In today's terms, the Waldo control harness is a motion capture suit. Rogers would gesticulate, and Waldo captured his movements and translated them to tape where it in turn could be converted into electrical pulses that operated the AA's. As Walt put it, "the operator of the harness has to be a bit of a ham actor." Rogers, who could be in the recording suit for hours at a time, recalled exaggerating his movements while programming the AA's. "I had to overreact in the harness to get the right movements in the figure." The added challenge was that AA programming had to be completed in one take; the recording tape could not be spliced and edited like a movie. Rogers burnished his AA skills with the ambitious Hall of Presidents at the Magic Kingdom and eventually became the art director for the park. Marty Sklar recalls that Rogers always had a solution for any problems that arose at Walt Disney World.

Like other first-generation Imagineers, Rogers worked closely with Walt. "We put forth our utmost effort, hoping to find the solution and please him. When we thought it was finished, we would show it to Walt and he'd say, 'that's coming along fine. You've got a good start there. Keep working at it.' And we were back to the drawing board. By requesting something impossible, he got improvements every time."

For his contributions to AA technology, Wathel Rogers was named a Disney Legend in 1995.

# SINGERS,
# SONGWRITERS
# AND COMPOSERS

The Disney Legends program honors those who have made significant contributions to The Walt Disney Company. Many recipients trace their heritage to the golden era of Disney feature length animation, or the early day of Imagineering, whose members created Disneyland and the modern theme park. However, there are plenty of recipients who have made more recent contributions to the company, particularly in the realm of musical theater. Beginning with *The Little Mermaid*, released in 1989 and throughout the 1990's, Disney enjoyed a renaissance in animation largely on the strength of timeless songs and melodies. Just as the Disney soundtrack of the 1960's was dominated by Richard and Robert Sherman, the 90's belongs to a handful of musical geniuses.

Perhaps no other musician personifies the contemporary Disney song better than Alan Menken. His contributions in this era are broad and impressive - *The Little Mermaid, Beauty and the Beast, Aladdin, Pocahontas, The Hunchback of Notre Dame* and *Hercules*. His ability to shift tone and style effortlessly help to propel and enhance the stories of Arielle, Belle and Jasmine, to name a few.

As a child, Menken was drawn to music and seemed pre-ordained to be a composer; he was tutored by piano and violin teachers but seemed more interested in creating his own musical pieces than practicing what he was assigned. He eventually fulfilled his potential, graduating from New York University with a degree in music. He remained in the world of musical theater in New York City and caught his big break when the off-Broadway production of *Little Shop of Horrors* became a cult hit. His music, and his lyricist partner Howard Ashman, were now hot property. Menken, along with Ashman, joined the Disney production of *The Little Mermaid*, composing such modern classics as "Part of Your World." Menken teamed again with Ashman on the next animated classic *Beauty and the Beast* complete with "Belle," a form-breaking extensive opening number that established the characters, story and tone for the film. Disney feature animation was on a roll and followed up with *Aladdin*, featuring Menken's energetic "Friend Like Me." He continues to write hit songs for Disney films including "Colors of the Wind" from *Pocahontas* and "Out There" from *The Hunchback of Notre Dame*. His prolific songwriting talent earned him eight Academy Awards in the Best Score and Best Song categories. When asked about thoughts on his songwriting, he replied "(y)ou should be able to understand not only the feeling, but the content of the song, just by hearing the music and not even the lyrics. What you're trying to say should be that clear."

Musical composition is half of the equation to creating memorable songs. Artfully crafted lyrics are necessary to move the story forward and showcase character exposition. Howard Ashman skillfully served as the muse to Menken's songs, collaborating with him on *The Little Mermaid, Beauty and the Beast and Aladdin* before his death, at age 40, of AIDS. His untimely departure necessitated Menken to collaborate with other wordsmiths, but while on these projects Ashman's work shined brightly.

Ashman seemed destined for musical theater following his Master of Fine Arts degree where he struck out for New York City to make his mark. Like so many others, his journey was not an overnight success but with Menken, their breakthrough came from *Little Shop of Horrors*. Ashman was a passionate believer in his Disney projects, including his choreography of how Sebastian should be animated during the infectious "Under the Sea" number from *The Little Mermaid*. His masterful command of the scene invoked memories of how Walt Disney himself pitched stories and scenes to his writers and animators.

Sir Tim Rice masterfully helped to fill the void following Ashman's death, contributing lyrics to *Beaty and the Beast, Aladdin* and the next Disney blockbuster, *The Lion King*. Rice too was steeped in musical theater, hailing from London stages where he had collaborated with Andrew Lloyd Webber on several classics including *Evita*. Rice joined the Disney fold in 1991 when he began working with Menken on *Beauty and the Beast*.

However, Rice's best work would be featured in *The Lion King*. Along with fellow Briton Sir Elton John, they crafted the richly textured songs including the epic "Circle of Life." Rice describes his songwriting style as breaking down the character's core components and building up verses from the pieces. For example, he noted that the lyrics for "I Just Can't Wait to Be King" should match the character. "Basically, I was just thinking of children playing games. Whatever they say has to be plausible. We knew the song was sung by (Simba as) a lion cub, so it had to be innocent, boppy and poppy."

Rice's musical counterpart for *The Lion King*, Sir Elton John, is no stranger to grand musical stages. He's a notable rock and pop icon from the 1970's and 80's, where his impressive body of work yielded thirty-five gold and twenty-five platinum albums. His live stage shows were a spectacle in which he graced the stage in outrageous sequined costumes. In the 90's, John made the transition from the rock stage to the silver screen when he partnered with Rice on the songs for *The Lion King*. John's additional masterpieces from the film include "Be Prepared," "Hakuna Matata" and "Can You Feel the Love Tonight." The latter composition earned John and Rice an Academy Award Oscar for Best Original Song in March, 1995. John, in his acceptance speech, completed the circle by dedicating the award to his grandmother Ivy Sewell, who had just recently passed away. "She was the one who sat me down at the piano when I was three and made me play. So I'm accepting this in her honor."

Disney Feature Animation continued generating hits in the 1990's and sought out new creative veins for the music. For *Tarzan*, another rock musician from England was brought in to put his unique spin on the score. Phil Collins generated new classics such as "Strangers Like Me" and "You'll Be In My Heart" which netted him an Academy Award Oscar in 2000 for Best Original Song. Collins' musical background includes elements as both musician and the

percussionist for Genesis and then as the band's lead singer. He parlayed this into a wildly successful solo career. The next logical step was to write songs for film. His 1985 ballad "Take A Look at Me Now" from *Against All Odds* earned him his first Oscar. Collins not only wrote the songs for *Tarzan* but also for *Brother Bear* several years later.

Songs from animated films, if done properly to elevate the story and characters, can have a profound legacy. The Disney animation renaissance in the 1990's perfectly crystalizes this notion. for their collective musical prowess, Alan Menken, Howard Ashman, Sir Tim Rice, Sir Elton John and Phil Collins have all been named Disney Legends.

# JODI BENSON

## 2011

What creates the staying power of a classic Disney animated character? Why does a wooden marionette who becomes a little boy still tug on heartstrings, decade after decade? How does a seemingly mismatched pair of canines stir the embers of love that resonates still today? How does a boy who never grows up create universal excitement in kids and a wistful remembrance in adults? How does a mermaid, confined to life under the waves, come to find true love and a happily ever after life? The answers, most likely, are unique and highly personal to every Disney fan. However, they all contain certain key ingredients: a character with relatable traits, animation and draftsmanship that is crisp and timeless, and opulent spoken and sung voices that crackle with warmth, strength, and courage. Ariel, the courageous mermaid, and star of *The Little Mermaid*, clearly excels in all categories. This film, released over a quarter century ago, ushered in the second renaissance of Disney animation and turned Jodi Benson, the speaking and singing voice of Ariel, into a national treasure.

Benson was born in Rockford, Illinois in 1961, the same year Disney released *One Hundred and One Dalmatians* and *The Parent Trap*. Her natural singing abilities were apparent at the early age of five. Says Benson of her childhood, "I just started singing and it was there, and I've been singing ever since." For college she stayed in Illinois and attended Millikin University with aspirations of law school. Instead, she earned a Bachelor of Fine Arts in musical theater. The legal world's loss turned out to be musical theater's gain. Benson set her sights on the Great White Way of Broadway and made her debut in 1983 in *Marilyn: An American Fable*. She next starred in the Howard Ashman and Marvin Hamlisch musical *Smile*. Perhaps as a precursor to her Disney career ahead of her, this musical featured Benson displaying her full vocal range on the sentimental ballad "Disneyland."

It was this collaboration with Ashman that led Benson to audition for *The Little Mermaid*. When *Smile* abruptly ended, Ashman, who was already beginning pre-production work on *The Little Mermaid*, encouraged Benson to audition for the movie. Benson, at the time, was skeptical about voice acting. "Nobody really wanted to do those types of jobs . . . My goal was to do Broadway musicals. Voice acting was something I didn't know anything about!" All auditions, including Benson's, were anonymous and the directors John Musker and Ron Clements had final say on their selection, The clarity and golden tones of Benson's voice ultimately won over the directors and she earned the role of Ariel.

Benson, again, was able to work with lyricist Ashman on a new project. Recalled Benson, "My fondest memories probably working with Howard Ashman in the studio and just having his direction and his guiding force. Just being so confident to know I was in good hands with him." One of the most challenging elements of portraying Ariel was the finding the right balance between speaking and singing as Ariel, particularly on the film's centerpiece song "Part of Your World." Clements, Musker and Ashman carefully guided Benson through the song. Said Benson of this process, "The passes and the selects they chose are not perfectly sung - some of them are not sung at all, some of them are spoken words, some of them are not held out, there's no vibrato, some of them are not the right note. The first time I heard it, I was like, 'Oh, that's not a perfect musical selection.' And they're like, 'No, that's what we did not want. We just wanted it to be real.'"

When it was released in1989 *The Little Mermaid* would mark the majestic return of Disney animation and ultimately earn over $200 million in ticket sales, and the Howard Ashman, Alan Menken calypso-inspired song "Under the Sea" would capture an Academy Award in 2000 for Best Original song.

The immediate, and ultimately long-term, success of *The Little Mermaid* caught Benson by pleasant surprise. She recently recalled, "I had no idea it was going to have such an impact until after the New York premiere. Seeing and hearing… wow… how people responded to it, I just couldn't believe it. We really thought we just did this project and it would disappear and go back and life would just be the way it was and it's never been the same since."

Benson would reprise her role as Ariel in additional Disney ventures, including Mickey's PhilharMagic at the Magic Kingdom, the brief television series also named *The Little Mermaid*, the direct-to-video sequel *The Little Mermaid 2: Return to the Sea*, and video game offerings Kingdom Hearts and Kinect Disneyland Adventures.

Benson, who initially eschewed voiceover work, would go on to do voice characters for Disney well beyond that of Ariel. Perhaps her second most recognized character is Barbie, from *Toy Story 2* and *Toy Story 3*, and the animated short *Toy Story Toons: Hawaiian Vacation*. She performed as Sam in the whimsical live action and animation comedy *Enchanted,* and as Helen of Troy for the *Hercules* television series and in *Hercules: Zero to Hero*.

In 2011, Benson was named a Disney Legend at the D23 Expo Disney Legends awards ceremony in Anaheim, California for her portrayal of Ariel.

# GEORGE BRUNS

## 2001

The Disney experience. It's something Disney fans around the globe know about intimately. It's the tingling sensation one gets when seeing the iconic castle or the Pixar lamp before a Disney film. It's hearing the goose bump-inducing whistle from the "Roger E. Broggie" at the Magic Kingdom. It's the scent of fresh citrus that triggers a memory of a fanciful flight aboard Soarin'. It's the rich texture of the various bells in the Expedition Everest queue and the unique chimes they produce. The Disney experience plays upon all the senses. Sound is a major factor, ranging from songs known by heart to film and television scores, and background music in the parks. Disney songwriters Richard and Robert Sherman are household names, but many other individuals have contributed to the vast array of the Disney sound. George Bruns may not be a recognized name to the casual Disney fan, but his wide body of music is. During his eighteen-year career with The Walt Disney Company, he composed and arranged music for animation, live-action, television and the parks. His work spans generations and has a timeless appeal.

George Bruns was destined to be a musician. As a child, he was a prodigy on the piano and soon after mastered the trombone and tuba. He enrolled at Oregon State Agricultural College (now Oregon State University) in 1932 to study engineering. However, he repeatedly fell back on his love of music, when he performed with the campus ROTC band and a local orchestra. "That's what I really enjoyed doing," he later recalled. He dropped out of college to pursue music full time in the Portland area.

As his musical talent grew, so too did his ambition. He left for the shining lights of Los Angeles in 1949, performing in jazz bands and nightclubs. Within these circles, he met fellow trombonist Ward Kimball, who happened to be an animator for Disney. In 1953, Kimball recommended Bruns to UPA, another animation company, who was looking for a jazz tuba performer for its animated short, "Little Boy with a Big Horn." With this move, Bruns successfully transitioned to Hollywood.

At the time, Disney was working on its third animated fairy tale, *Sleeping Beauty*. For Walt, it was to be a masterpiece, utilizing the talents of all Nine Old Men. The art direction was more striking and articulate when compared to *Snow White and the Seven Dwarfs* and *Cinderella*. The score for *Sleeping Beauty*, based on the ballet of the same name by famed Russian composer Tschaikovsky, was to elevate the film as well. On the strength of Kimball's recommendation, Bruns, in 1953, was brought in to compose the soundtrack. His film peers were equally impressed; Bruns was nominated for an Academy Award for Best Scoring of a Musical Picture in 1959, when the long-developing film was released.

Bruns remained with Disney as a musical director and skillfully aided the company as it entered the new arena of television. Disney had an instant hit in 1954 with Davy Crockett, and the studio quickly worked to maximize its potential. While editing the filmed material, it was discovered there wasn't enough footage for full television episodes. Walt suggested some filler material be produced and an accompanying song. Serendipity struck, as Bruns' song "The Ballad of Davy Crockett" became a hit beyond all expectation. It was written in short order on a tight production schedule, but the show producer, Bill Walsh, wasn't happy with it. Walt gave the song his blessing, proving again his unique talent of understanding the American public. The hit single sold over ten million copies. Disney had another successful television live-action show with *Zorro*, which aired from 1957 to 1959. Bruns created a swashbuckling theme song that crackled with energy. Disney's entry into the variety show field was the groundbreaking *Mickey Mouse Club* show, which ran from 1955 to 1958. Bruns contributed several songs to the show, including the Friday show theme Talent Round-Up, a Western hoe down that would make Woody and Jessie proud.

Film scores for shorts and feature length films were Bruns' strong suit. Following his success with *Sleeping Beauty*, he composed a wide variety of music that reflected the subject at hand. His notable work includes the patriotic theme for *Johnny Tremain* and the lighthearted fare for *The Absent-Minded Professor* and its sequel, *Son of Flubber*. His jazz roots shined through on his compositions for *One Hundred and One Dalmatians* and *The AristoCats*. His score for *The Love Bug* and *Herbie Rides Again* is nimble and mod, befitting the impish title character. His hypnotic score for *The Jungle Book* is silky smooth; the soft vibrato of the overture's bass flute perfectly sets the scene for mystery and intrigue. Disney historians with a keen ear will note that the overture is a repurposing of Bruns' earlier work for the 1964 New York World's Fair, from the WED-designed attraction Ford's Magic Skyway. In addition to his score for *Sleeping Beauty*, Bruns received three additional Academy Award nominations: his arrangements for *Babes in Toyland*, *The Sword in the Stone*, and the song "Love" from *Robin Hood*. Additionally, he wrote the music for several animated shorts, most notably the swinging "Humphrey Hop" from *In the Bag*, featuring Humphrey the Bear.

Bruns' influence isn't just limited to television and film. Disneyland and Walt Disney World fans can thank him for lasting contributions to the parks. Pirates of the Caribbean opened at Disneyland in 1967 and in the Magic Kingdom in 1973 and remains an iconic Disney attraction to this day. A significant reason for its popularity is its timeless theme song, "Yo Ho (A Pirates Life for Me)." Imagineer Xavier Atencio, the show writer for the attraction, composed the song lyrics to the score that Bruns composed. Bruns and Atencio collaborated again on "Bear Band Serenade," the opening number to the Country Bear Jamboree. Bruns also wrote the music for the attraction's closing song "Come Again (Come On In)."

Bruns' music is also a part of the Magic Kingdom's past. Adventureland's original counter service restaurant was the Adventureland Verandah, which offered a unique blend of Caribbean, Asian, African, and Polynesian styles and cuisine. The restaurant closed, however, in 1994 but the building remains available for character meet and greets and other special events, until late 2015 when the Jungle Navigation Co. LTD Skipper Canteen restaurant opened. When the Adventureland Verandah was in operation, its background music loop included a few tracks from Bruns' *Moonlight Time in Old Hawaii* album. The soothing, island-inspired songs were a welcome treat to park guests weary from crisscrossing the Magic Kingdom.

Like many Disney veterans of the 1950's and 60's, Bruns had the opportunity to work directly with Walt. He later recalled, "Walt was always very good to me personally. He pretty much let me go my own way, trusting my own musical sense of what was right. The one thing about him that really impressed me was his fantastic memory for detail." It seems fitting that Bruns participated in the last project Walt did – the EPCOT film he completed just one more before Walt's premature death. The twenty-four-minute film outlined Walt's ambition for an experimental prototype city of tomorrow. The background music for the film was done by Bruns and his musical Disney colleague, Buddy Baker. Together, their score highlighted many recurring musical themes from Disney's work at the 1964 New York World's Fair and the *Disneyland* television show.

Bruns retired from The Walt Disney Company in 1976 and returned to his native Oregon. He passed away in 1983 and was posthumously named a Disney Legend in 2001.

# LEGENDS OF DISNEY FILMS

Disney is synonymous with many terms. The first that come to mind are animation, theme parks and movies. The silver screen is one of the company's best ways to showcase its talent of writers, directors, actors, and other unique skillsets. With Disney's movie history, it's only natural that several Disney Legends have earned their right to that title via work done for Disney films.

# PETER ELLENSHAW
## 1993

Live-action films require the collective effort of many to create cinematic masterpieces. Writers and directors let their imagination run wild, and the cast of actors and actresses bring characters to life, from script pages to the screen. Art and costume directors work in tandem, adding depth and layers to the film. Producers have the arduous task of keeping the production on schedule and, more importantly, on budget. In this context, directors often rely on visual effects to achieve results they cannot obtain. Matte artists are called upon to magically create never-seen-before environments or recreate sets of bygone times and places. These artists are responsible for some of Hollywood's most iconic scenes, such as the seemingly never-ending warehouse that concludes *Raiders of the Lost Ark* and the dystopian ending to *Planet of the Apes,* that features the unexpected reveal of the Statue of Liberty. Before green screens and computer graphics technology became widely used in filmmaking, art directors often relied on mattes, large paintings on glass, that could be incorporated into the filming production. Peter Ellenshaw is one of Hollywood's most gifted matte artists, and he enjoyed an amazing thirty-year career with The Walt Disney Company as an artist.

Ellenshaw was born in Sussex, England in 1913. At a young age, he discovered his interest and talent in drawing. As a teenager, he found it necessary to financially support his family, but he maintained his passion for art on the side. Fate directed him to an encounter with renowned matte artist Percy Day, who steered the young Ellenshaw into the film business. He soon became skilled artisan in this field. His early works include *The Thief of Baghdad, The Red Shoes* and *Black Narcissus.*

Like so many other Disney Legends, how Ellenshaw came to be employed by Walt Disney is a fascinating story. During World War II, The Walt Disney Studio had overseas profits in England that were frozen and available only for use there, due to that country's financial quota laws. Disney took this as an opportunity to film in England for the company's first live action feature, *Treasure Island,* released in 1950. Walt utilized an English cast and crew, and matte artist Ellenshaw was the natural choice, who eagerly jumped at the opportunity. "I hadn't thought of working for Disney. He was an animator. But when my chance came, I grabbed it," recalled Ellenshaw. He created about forty mattes for the film, notably of the sailing ships in London harbor and other wide-angle scenes too difficult to recreate with actual sets. Disney went on to create additional films in England in the ensuing years and Ellenshaw's artistry was used for each one. A formidable alliance was created.

Ellenshaw relocated to Burbank to continue his career with Disney, and his first domestic film is one of his masterworks. For *20,000 Leagues Under the Sea*, he created, on matte glass, Captain Nemo's exotic island Vulcania seen from multiple angles, including its volcanic interior lagoon. His other notable artistic and visual contributions to Disney films include *Darby O'Gill and the Little People, The Love Bug, Bedknobs and Broomsticks*, and television shows such as *Zorro* and *Davy Crockett.*

Ellenshaw reflected on the skill and artistry necessary to create an effective matte. "To judge a matte painting, you have to stand back where the camera is and make sure not to give it too much detail, just enough to fool the eye. Too much finish on it and it becomes static. It doesn't look quite real. One time, Walt was looking at one of my mattes and said, 'Looks like a painting' and all the guys started laughing thinking it was a joke but it wasn't. Walt was trying to tell me to put less into it, not in terms of quality, but detail so that it was the illusion of being real." This concept was brilliantly executed on Ellenshaw's pinnacle achievement for Disney: *Mary Poppins*. To wit, consider the multiple wide-angle scenes of Edwardian London, featuring birds-eye views of the Thames River, Big Ben, Buckingham Palace and other notable London locales. The set for the rooftop chimney sweep dance sequence utilized mattes, as well as the classic image of Mary Poppins, Bert, Jane and Michael climbing a makeshift staircase formed from black smoke. As film critic and movie historian Leonard

Maltin pointed out, "Peter was working his magic in Disney films. People never knew how he accomplished his visual feats. . . . and when you think that *Mary Poppins* was made without anyone ever setting foot outside a soundstage – let alone visiting London – you get some idea of what he was able to pull off." Appropriately, Ellenshaw earned an Academy Award for his visual effects on *Mary Poppins*. For Disney trivia fans, Ellenshaw made a fascinating contribution to the film. His recitation of the bawdy English dance song "Knees Up, Mother Brown" served as the inspiration to "Step in Time."

Ellenshaw's Disney contributions weren't limited to film and television. He also made notable contributions to Disneyland, particularly its early iteration of Tomorrowland. He aided with the design of the seventy-six-foot-tall TWA Moonliner. For Space Station X-1's fifty-mile-high placement, he created the likeness of satellite images of planet earth. His most lasting contribution to Walt's first theme park is the oversized aerial painting he made of Disneyland on a four-foot by eight-foot canvas. He even used luminescent paint so that, when featured under fluorescent light, it would mimic how the park would appear at night. The painting was such a hit that it was used on a widely successful postcard campaign to advertise the new park.

Ellenshaw retired from Disney following the 1979 release of *The Black Hole* but returned to work for the 1990 theatrical release *Dick Tracy*. His son, Harrison Ellenshaw, followed in his footsteps and became a matte artist himself, notably on *Star Wars: A New Hope*.

Like other artists who worked for Disney, Ellenshaw connected to Walt on a personal level. He recollected, "Walt had the ability to communicate with artists. He'd talk to you on your level – artist to artist. He used to say, 'I can't draw, Peter.' But he had the soul of an artist, and he had a wonderful way of transferring his enthusiasm to you."

For his artistic contributions to Disney films, television and the parks, Peter Ellenshaw was named a Disney Legend in 1993. He passed away on February 12, 2007.

# ROBERT STEVENSON

## 2002

The heritage of The Walt Disney Company began with animation, beginning with Oswald the Lucky Rabbit, Mickey Mouse, and the Silly Symphonies. The success of these animated shorts gave Walt and his animators the confidence that they could succeed with feature length animation, which they brilliantly accomplished in 1937 with *Snow White and the Seven Dwarfs*. Animated features were now the staple of Disney, and they continue to this day. But Walt wasn't always content to remain with the status quo. In the interest of pushing artistic and technical boundaries, he additionally directed the Studio into live action films, beginning with the period drama *Treasure Island*, released in 1950. Disney eventually branched into comedies, beginning with *The Shaggy Dog*. Across this wide range of material, from dramatic period films to whimsical musical and family comedies, there was consistency, satisfying generations of Disney film fans. Many of the screenplays of many of the early films were penned by Bill Walsh and Don DaGradi, who understood their audience. But perhaps the greatest level of consistency comes from the director, so it will come as no surprise to learn that many of the early live action films were directed by one man - Robert Stevenson. His Disney career spanned nearly twenty years, beginning with the drama *Johnny Tremain* in

1957 and ending with the comedy *The Shaggy D.A.* in 1976. In between, he directed a wide range of films for Disney, including dramas *Old Yeller* and *Kidnapped*. He smoothly handled fanciful pieces such as *Darby O'Gill and the Little People* and *Bedknobs and Broomsticks*. His strongest suit was for comedies, including many classics such as *The Absent-Minded Professor* and its sequel, *Son of Flubber*, *That Darn C*at!, *Blackbeard's Ghost*, *The Love Bug* and *Herbie Rides Again*. Of his twenty-one films he directed for Disney, one stands head and shoulders above the others, and is his crowning achievement: 1964's *Mary Poppins*, a fanciful blend of music, animation, drama and comedy about a practically perfect English nannie and the family she aids. So profound was the film and Stevenson's handling of it that it was nominated for Best Picture, and Stevenson for Best Director. Julie Andrews, in her film debut as Mary Poppins, was nominated for Best Actress and took home the Oscar.

Robert Stevenson, English by birth, was formally educated at Cambridge University studying science. However, it was a psychology assignment involving filmgoers that fortuitously steered him to a career in movies, first as a writer and ultimately as a director. After several years of work in England, he was recruited to Los Angeles by famed Hollywood producer David Selznick. His notable early achievement was *Jane Eyre*. Stevenson worked through the 1940's and early 1950's in Hollywood, but his latter Pre-Disney work was primarily in television, notably "Alfred Hitchcock Presents." Walt Disney Productions was also involved in the new medium of television and had a hit on its hands with *Zorro*. Stevenson was given the direction assignments on three episodes for *Zorro*. Walt was sufficiently impressed with his skills behind the lens and gave him the reins of Disney's live action film *Johnny Tremain*. It was a twofold success; the Colonial America drama proved to be a box office hit for Disney, and Stevenson proved he was up to Disney's standards. His follow up was the legendary *Old Yeller*. He next turned his attention to comedy with the *Shaggy Dog*. A new Disney star was born, albeit one behind the lens. He was especially prolific from 1960 to 1968, when the quiet and unassuming Stevenson capably directed a dozen features, providing a steady stream of hits.

Many of his films involved working with children, which can be challenging if they aren't sufficiently trained as actors. Not so with Stevenson. He worked with a young Tommy Kirk on his film debut in *Old Yeller*. Recalled Kirk, "I was lucky. I had the greatest director in the world, Robert Stevenson, this very quiet little Englishman. (He was) very patient, very good with kids. You do (acting) for your director. and so I just managed to bring up from within me whatever he needed."

Stevenson was also mindful of the financial aspect of films and the necessity of hewing to a budget. Years later, he recalled, "the (complex scenes) had to be storyboarded. I was on the pictures from the beginning, so I was consulted on everything. The storyboard kept the costs down. I first suggested the use of storyboards for live action on *Darby O'Gill*. The trick (shots) made it necessary. I asked Walt, 'how if I storyboarded this?' He was delighted."

*Mary Poppins* was a long developing project for Walt, which involved years of dogged pursuit for the film rights for Pamela Travers' work, a collection of books about the fanciful adventures of an English nannie. She finally relented, pending script approval, to hand her material over to Disney. Since her work was more a collection of short vignettes, an overall film script had to be created from the material. Veteran Disney writers Walsh and DaGradi, along with songwriters Richard and Robert Sherman, wrote the elaborate script. Julie Andrews was cast for the lead, after a personal visit and request from Walt following her Broadway performance in *Camelot*. Dick Van Dyke was cast as Bert the chimney sweep, based on his broad physical comedy skills. With the talented cast and crew, script and songs, Robert Stevenson stepped in and deftly directed a masterpiece, turning *Mary Poppins* into Disney's biggest live action hit, both commercially and critically. Personally, he made a modest contribution to the film. The books were set in 1930's England but the script altered it to 1910. Since Stevenson was a child in England at that time, he advised the set decorators about toys for the nursery room in the Banks' house.

Like many other Disney Studios veterans at the time, Stevenson had a personal relationship with Walt. He noted that Walt rewarded eagerness. Stevenson enthusiastically requested to direct *The Absent-Minded Professor*. He later recalled, "Walt believed in enthusiasm. . . . If you were as enthused as he was, he would give you the job." He further recalled, "I met Walt right from the start and always found him to be accessible. He never interfered with the director on the set. He always stood in the background. His view was there is nothing an outsider could do while the picture was filmed. He was close to the writing and editing but not to shooting."

While filming the comedy *Blackbeard's Ghost*, Walt paid a visit to the set in November 1966. It would be the last time he personally oversaw a Disney film. Stevenson remembered: "Suddenly I came onto the set and saw him sitting on one of those stools and he was drinking coffee. I said, 'Walt, I thought you were in the hospital.' He said, 'Yeah, well, they cut away my ribs to get to something.'" The biopsy results indicated that he was in the late stages of cancer. He passed away the following month.

Despite his broad success as a director, Stevenson remained humble, attributing a film's success to teamwork. He had a simple philosophy about his job - "When I'm directing a picture, what I have in mind is a happy audience, enjoying it in a movie house." For his contributions to The Walt Disney Company, Robert Stevenson was posthumously named a Disney Legend in 2002.

# Television Stars as Disney Legends

With one hundred years of entertainment offerings, The Walt Disney Company, rightly so, counts animation and theme parks among its significant pillars. Of no less significance is Disney's involvement in the medium of television. Animation and live-action feature releases were limited to several a year, and a visit to Anaheim or Orlando might be a once-in-a-lifetime vacation, but television offers a more intimate and repeatable avenue for Disney to entertain fans at home. Walt Disney wisely stepped into the arena of television programming in the 1950's, despite the conventional wisdom of the time that it would cannibalize his theatrical releases. Instead, Disney created vital new content for television that cemented the company as a critical source of programming. Walt, with the competent assistance of brother Roy, created symbiotic relationships with television partners that benefitted all parties. For ABC, the weekly anthology series *Walt Disney's Disneyland* gave ABC programming content that showcased the construction of Disneyland, whetting the nation's appetite and creating anticipation for the theme park. Several years later on NBC, the series *Walt Disney's Wonderful World of Colo*r brilliantly showcased the exciting potential of color television. RCA, an original manufacturer of color television sets, was owned by NBC, creating a mutually beneficial three-party alliance. Disney and television have been related ever since, particularly with Disney's ownership of ABC, ESPN, its own Disney Channel and the current streaming service Disney+. With this background, it's easy to understand that numerous Disney Legends owe that title to their years of service within the framework of television.

From its earliest days, television was a natural avenue for news. Print and radio sources of information could tell only part of the story, but television could present it with more layers - film and video footage now complemented news anchors behind a desk. For over twenty years, ABC's nightly news program, *World News Tonight*, enjoyed the talents of Peter Jennings (2006) who steadfastly reported the days' news with the analytical mindset of a globe-trotting reporter. Jennings joined ABC News in 1964 and earned his credentials while reporting from around the world. For his reporting and news anchor duties, Jennings deservedly earned sixteen Emmy Awards. Jennings passed away on August 7, 2005, in New York City.

For television news programs to be most effective, a talented executive behind the camera needs to be in charge. In that regard, Roone Arledge (2007) masterfully guided ABC not only in its news department, but also in sports programming. Arledge joined ABC in 1960 and retooled its sports broadcasting, refining the concept of sports as entertainment with the wildly successful *ABC's Wide World of Sports*, that utilized slow motion and instant replays to better engage the audience. Arledge notched another contribution to sports programming with the implementation of *Monday Night Football* in 1970. NFL action no longer was limited to Sunday afternoons. In 1977, Arledge was promoted to President of ABC News. Although he had no formal journalistic training, he recognized that ABC News talent needed room to shine, and in addition to Jennings at the anchor desk, he provided Sam Donaldson, Ted Koppel and David Brinkley with their own forums. Finally, Arledge gave voice to Barbara Walters (2008), who enjoyed a commanding presence on television.

Walters is best known today for insightful interviews with celebrities, world leaders and others she deems "fascinating," but she first earned her stripes as an intrepid news reporter for both NBC and CBS before joining ABC in 1976. She made international news the following year with a groundbreaking joint interview of Egypt's Anwar Sadat and Israel's Menachem

Begin, Middle East political adversaries. She shined on her own news show, *20/20*, and anchored the top-rated and always popular *The Barbara Walters Specials*, interviewing cultural luminaries. Walters continued her television presence as host of the daytime talk show, *The View* until her retirement from that forum. In addition to being a Disney Legend, Walters is a member of the Academy of Television Arts and Sciences Hall of Fame. Walters passed away December 30, 2022.

The medium of television is ideally suited for entertainment, and in this regard, Dick Clark (2013) perfectly embodies the spirit of exuberance. Clark's television career spanned nearly fifty years, beginning with the homegrown Philadelphia show *Bandstand*, which became a syndicated national hit program *American Bandstand,* which featuring live musical acts and dancing teens. His show helped establish classic artists such as Chuck Berry, James Brown, and Buddy Holly. With the clout achieved from *American Bandstand,* which ran for over thirty years, Clark created his own television production company and branched into a variety of formats, such as daytime gameshows including *Pyramid* and prime time variety

programming including *Bloopers & Practical Jokes*. To an older generation, Clark is synonymous with *American Bandstand*, and for younger viewers he's equally known for hosting the annual *Dick Clark's New Years Rockin' Eve* on ABC, which ran from 1973 to 2011. All told, Clark produced over 7,500 hours of television programming. Clark suffered from a stroke in December 2004 and was unable to host the show on New Year's Eve 2004. Instead, Regis Philbin hosted that event. Ryan Seacrest of *America's Got Talent* fame eventually took over the hosting duties. Clark returned the following year, but the debilitating effects of his stroke were still apparent. Clark died in 2012 at the age of 82.

Finally, a discussion of Disney and television wouldn't be complete without a review of stars created on behalf of original studio content - Fess Parker (1991), for his portrayal of

American pioneer Davy Crockett, and original Mousketeers Jimmy Dodd (1992) and Annette Funicello (1992), from the *Mickey Mouse Club* television show.

Parker became an overnight sensation for his honest and gritty portrayal of Crockett and helped launch a national craze for coonskin caps and public recitations of "The Ballad of Davy Crockett." Parker's portrayal of Crockett lasted for only three lengthy television shows, but he forever lives in American lore of frontier times. Parker would later portray another American icon on the small screen when he took on the persona of Daniel Boone, which ran for six seasons on NBC, from 1964 to 1970.

Disney's other breakout television program was the *Mickey Mouse Club* show. The original series, which ran from 1955 to 1959, was a daily variety show that featured a cast of young men and women dubbed Mouseketeers, and an adult leader, or Head Mouseketeer, Jimmie Dodd.

Dodd was a gifted singer, songwriter, and guitarist whose natural affability made him perfect for the show. Through his friendship with Disney animator (and future Legend) Bill Justice, Dodd wrote a song for the show and performed it personally for Walt. That performance, an audition of sorts, convinced Walt that Dodd was a perfect match for the program. Dodd wrote over thirty songs for the show, including the energetic title piece "Mickey Mouse Club March." Dodd passed away on November 10, 1964, in Honolulu, Hawaii.

If Dodd was the adult star of the show, then Annette Funicello was the breakaway child star. The young starlet was hand-picked by Walt after he observed her in a local production of *Swan Lake*. Although she was just twelve at the time, Walt observed in her poise and grace beyond her young age. For four years, Funicello brought her singing, dancing, and acting talents to the show.

In addition to the *Mickey Mouse Club*, Funicello starred in other Disney television shows such as *Zorro*, *Adventures in Dairyland* and *Spin and Marty*. Her Disney career wasn't limited to the small screen; she starred in Disney films such as *The Shaggy Dog*, and with her singing talents, she recorded fifteen albums for Walt Disney Records. Notable hits include "Tall Paul" and "How Will I Know My Love." She passed away April 8, 2013 from complications related to multiple fibrosis.

Many Disney Legends earned a portion of their award due to their work on Television, but the collective works of Peter Jennings, Roone Arledge, Barbara Walters, Dick Clark, Fess Parker, Jimmie Dodd, and Annette Funicello shows how they mastered the art of television.

# VOICE ARTISTS

# PAUL FREES

## 2006

In the Disney family there are countless Legends whose faces may be unknown, but they are renowned for their timeless work. Animators create cinematic masterpieces, and Imagineers fabricate fantastical attractions that can, quite literally, whisk us away to Neverland. Voice artists play an equally important role in the Disney experience, adding a critical sonic layer to films, animated shorts and Disney theme park attractions. In this regard, the collective works of Paul Frees shine brightly. His silky baritone has graced the silver screen, the television set and classic attractions at both Disneyland and Walt Disney World.

Paul Frees was born in Chicago on June 22, 1920, and raised in a pre-television era where radio was king. He began an early career in this medium, and his versatility and knack for capturing style, nuance and pitch with his voice allowed him to filter to the top of radio stars. His career in radio began in 1942 but was briefly interrupted when he was drafted into the United States Army. He was injured while serving his country at Normandy on D Day and returned home to recuperate. Under the GI Bill, he briefly enrolled at the Chouinard Art Institute (which later morphed into the California Institute of the Arts at the direction of Walt and Roy Disney), but eventually dropped out. He remained in the Los Angeles area, continuing his work in radio on several noted serials and eventually into film. As a measure of his value to the industry, he was often tasked with recreating the voice work of others when necessary, during film post-production. For example, Frees dubbed for Japanese actor Toshiro Mifune when he appeared in English language films. Said Mifune, "Paul sounds more like me than I do."

Frees' chameleon-like voice and his instinct to capture the spirit and heart of a character led to his wide appearance on animation serials and specials through the 1960's and 1970's. He was a regular performer for animator Jay Ward, including notable performances as Boris Badenov, the nemesis on the *Rocky and Bullwinkle Show*, and Inspector Fenwick from *Dudley Do-Right*. He also was featured prominently on Rankin/Bass Productions, a studio which created stop-motion seasonal specials such as *Santa Claus is Comin' to Town, Frosty the Snowman,* and *Frosty's Winter Wonderland*. Fans of these specials will recall his work in them as Burgermeister Meisterburger, Santa Claus, and Jack Frost, respectively. His golden intonations weren't limited to television programs but also to its advertisements. In this regard, he is famous for his performances as Toucan Sam for Froot Loops and Poppin' Fresh, the Pillsbury Doughboy.

Frees was in high demand in Hollywood where he provided voice work for numerous studios, which naturally included Walt Disney Productions. He started his Disney career by narrating various episodes of Disney's television programs such as "Man In Space." He also narrated the 1959 comedy *Shaggy Dog*, and even made a rare on-screen cameo in the film as Dr. J. W. Galvin. A discussion of Disney history would not be complete without covering animation, and here Frees has a prominent entry. He provided the eccentric and entertaining voice and persona of Professor Ludwig Von Drake, a highly educated European mallard and uncle to Donald Duck. Frees brought Von Drake to life in eighteen Disney television specials, beginning in "An Adventure In Color" on the premiere episode of *Walt Disney's Wonderful World of Color*.

The Disney theme park experience is full of sights and sounds that stay with guests long after the vacation is over, and here again Paul Frees' contributions are vast and memorable at Disneyland, Walt Disney World and even Disney's attractions at the 1964-65 New York World's Fair. Walt Disney's precursor to Imagineering was WED Industries, and it created several state-of-the-art attractions for the Fair, including Great Moments with Mr. Lincoln for the state of Illinois pavilion. The show featured a never-before seen Audio-Animatronic figure of President Lincoln. Paul Frees provided the somber narration and introduction to the show. His same role was also featured at Disneyland when Great Moments with Mr. Lincoln premiered there in 1965. Frees' presidential credits don't end with Lincoln. When Walt Disney World opened in 1971, one of its signature attractions was the Hall of Presidents, featuring the likeness of every Commander-in-Chief and updated accordingly. The original program that ran from 1971 through 1993 featured a stirring film highlighting critical moments in American history as a precursor to the presidential AA's. Frees showed his versatility in this film, taking on the vocal roles of George Washington, Stephen Douglas and colonial era Pennsylvania Governor Thomas Mifflin. He also provided additional ancillary voices in the film.

Disney theme parks are constantly in a state of growth and change. As Walt said, "Disneyland will never be completed. It will continue to grow as long as there is imagination left in the world." Part of this process includes older attractions making way newer adventures. In this context, Paul Frees has another notable entry in his Disney resume, as the narrator of the Disneyland classic Adventures Through Inner Space, the park's first Omnimover attraction which opened in 1967. It closed twenty years later, yielding to Star Tours.

These accomplishments alone are enough for an impressive Disney career. But Frees has two other contributions to the Disney parks that elevate his stature tenfold. First is Pirates of the Caribbean, the swashbuckling spectacular that debuted in Anaheim in 1967 and Orlando in 1973. Frees voices the mysterious, unseen pirate that intones "dead men tell no tales" as guests begin their journey. Few of the scalawags have names, save for the addition of Jack Sparrow, but all Disney fans know who the auctioneer is. Frees brings this rogue to life as he barks out "I'm not spongin' for rum. It be gold I'm after!" The Haunted Mansion is the other classic Disney E-ticket attraction that prominently features Frees. As guests enter the stretching room, before climbing into a Doom Buggies, they are greeted by the Ghost Host, the mischievous resident speaking in a ghoulish, disembodied voice. Frees' delicious intonation of "welcome, foolish mortals, to the Haunted Mansion" simultaneously chills and thrills guests as they journey through the manor. Frees recorded his rich voice work over forty years ago and it remains intact to this day, effectively immortalizing him in the Haunted Mansion alongside the nine-hundred, ninety-nine happy haunts. What a tribute to a legendary career.

Paul Frees remained active in Hollywood until 1986, when he passed away at the age of sixty-six. For his contributions to The Walt Disney Company, he was posthumously named a Disney Legend in 2006.

# STERLING HOLLOWAY

**1991**

Disney fans around the world have, for decades, come to know and love the characters and stories that unfold on the silver screen, the widescreen television, the portable DVD player or the mobile device and now streaming services such as Disney+. Large or small, there's something extraordinary about seeing Mickey Mouse, Cinderella, Mulan or Sheriff Woody, to name a few, come to life. Enveloped in richly detailed worlds that burst with color and song, fans remember, time and again, favorite characters as they span their own personal arcs. Music enhances the experience, sometimes leaving us to, quite literally, whistle while we work. But what isn't always so obvious is the countless number of dedicated individuals it takes to bring the animated magic to life. Writers, story board artists, animators, including the laborious ink and paint process, editors, musicians, and many more are necessary to breathe life into the animated feature. However, the one element that perhaps best resonates with the audience is the work of the voice actors. These men, women and children bring depth of emotion and nuance to their vocalization. They must become the character onscreen, heard but not seen. Guests leaving the theater may not know the face of the humans behind the animated characters, but they certainly best remember their contributions.

The Disney Legends program has honored multiple individuals who have worked as voice artists. The list includes, but is not limited to - Pinto Colvig and Clarence Nash, the original voices of Goofy and Donald Duck, respectively; Adriana Caselotti, the youthful and exuberant voice of Snow White; Cliff Edwards, eternally known for his work as Jiminy Cricket, and Tim Allen, the boisterous voice of Buzz Lightyear of the Toy Story franchise. For his body of work, however, one Disney voice artist stands above the others - Sterling Holloway. His is not a household name, but Kaa, the Cheshire Cat and the unflappable Winnie the Pooh certainly are. Sterling Holloway brought all three to life with his highly distinctive voice.

Holloway enjoyed a fifty-year career in Hollywood that spanned radio, television, and film. Born and raised in rural Georgia, he enrolled in the American Academy of Dramatic Arts in New York City at the tender age of fifteen. It seems he knew that he was destined for a thespian career. He honed his craft early in the theatre before heading to Los Angeles in 1926, three years after Walt made his fateful trip west. Holloway's first film was a silent comedy, common from the era. Hollywood was in a period of transition, and soon "talkies" were literally the talk of the town. With his red pompadour and uniquely high-pitched and slightly raspy voice, Holloway easily made the transition to sound films. His smooth transition mirrored that of Walt Disney, who deftly moved from shorts to feature films, and eventually into television and live action, keeping the Disney company fresh and current.

Holloway's Disney career nearly began with Walt's breakthrough feature *Snow White and the Seven Dwarfs*. Walt himself had been closely following Holloway's film career, and in 1934 penciled him in as the voice of Sleepy. That role ultimately went to Pinto Colvig. Disney didn't forget him, and Holloway made his Disney debut in a brief but memorable scene in *Dumbo*, as Mr. Stork delivering a pint-sized pachyderm to Mrs. Jumbo. Next, he voiced the adult incarnation of Flower the skunk in *Bambi*. Although his initial roles were small, his mellifluous voice, with its gentle southern drawl still peeking through, led Disney producers and directors to cast him in a new light: he would serve as a narrator of short films, his voice lending a comforting credence to the audience. His first narration was as Professor Holloway describing the life of Pablo the penguin in Disney's second South American Goodwill Tour package film, *The Three Caballeros*. The next package film - *Make Mine Music* - featured an animated adaption of the classic orchestral piece *Peter and the Wolf*. Holloway's light-hearted narration offered an effective counterweight to the frightening antagonist. He additionally narrated Disney classic shorts *The Little House*, a sweet-hearted story of a simple home that stands the test of time, and *Susie the Little Blue Coupe*, whose anthropomorphic styling of automobiles was the source of inspiration to Pixar for the *Cars* movies.

Holloway's voice work with these movies and shorts had cemented his reputation within the

Disney company, but his best work was ahead of him. The studio was ambitiously adapting Lewis Carroll's *Alice in Wonderland* for its next animated feature. The film was filled with marvelous, mysterious, and fanciful characters, including the Mad Hatter, the White Rabbit, the Queen of Hearts, and of course Alice. However, perhaps the most memorable character is the Cheshire Cat. Holloway's silky performance as the curiously philosophical feline is frequently lauded as the film's highlight.

*The Jungle Book*, released in 1967, is cited as the last animated feature that Walt Disney personally supervised. Holloway was cast as Kaa the python at the personal request of Walt. Holloway recalled, "Walt was a stickler for voices. He came to me and said, 'When you've finished what you're doing today... See what you can do with the snake. I can't find the right voice.' So I went in and decided to make Kaa have a distinct ache in his back." Holloway's supporting work as Kaa was widely praised. Disney historian Jim Fanning noted about the performance: "Holloway not only delivered the lines with a mixture of menace and misplaced self-confidence but also ad-libbed dialogue that sparked the imaginations of the artists." Walt was so pleased with Holloway's initial work that he urged for Kaa to be added back later into the film, for a confrontation with the film's other antagonist, Shere Khan.

Holloway, in the twilight of his Disney career, had saved his best for last. The Disney company, between 1966 and 1974, released three whimsical featurettes based on the A. A. Milne character Winnie the Pooh and his Hundred Acre Wood companions - *Winnie the Pooh and the Honey Tree*, *Winnie the Pooh and the Blustery Day*, and *Winnie the Pooh and Tigger Too*. Holloway's soft and sweet raspy voice was perfect for the manifestation of the "bear of very little brain," whose simple and singular goal is honey.

Holloway, for the first time at Disney, played a leading role instead of a supporting part, allowing him the opportunity to let his full range of acting and singing skills shine. He was the perfect embodiment of Pooh as he delicately sang "I'm Just a Little Black Rain Cloud," the infectious Sherman brothers' song that highlighted the first featurette. Holloway cited Winnie the Pooh as his favorite character, which should come as no surprise. Following the enormous success of the films, the two became synonymous with each other. Appropriately enough, Winnie the Pooh served as Sterling Holloway's escort when he was awarded the Disney Legends honor in 1991.

# JACK WAGNER

## 2005

So many favorite attractions and shows at Walt Disney World are rich in details that stay with guests long after they have returned home. Iconic phrases help to extend a timeless quality to Disney theme parks. "Welcome, foolish mortals" quickly conjures images of Doom Buggies swirling through the Haunted Mansion. Mention Pirates of the Caribbean, and "dead men tell no tales" surely comes to mind. For those seeking adventure, perhaps "this here's the wildest ride in the wilderness!" will bring a quick smile as they recollect the rollicking adventures of Big Thunder Mountain Railroad. Fans of Disney's nightly fireworks pageants will immediately visualize bursts of color over Cinderella Castle when they hear "star light, star bright. First star I see tonight." However, not all iconic Disney phrases are affiliated with attractions or shows, or even inside a park. One of the most-repeated phrases, so simple yet timeless, is from the monorail that whisks guests around Walt Disney World - "Please stand clear of the doors. Por favor manténgase alejado de las puertas." The man behind that cheerful, silky voice is Disney Legend Jack Wagner, a gifted voiceover artist who spent three decades as the official park announcer for Disneyland, as well as other Disney theme parks and productions.

Wagner was born December 17, 1925, to French-born parents. his bilingual household allowed him to get an early start in show business, when he dubbed English speaking movies into French, for foreign markets. He discovered at this tender age that voice was the key to future success. He also turned his attention to the business side of Hollywood, working as a contract actor at MGM while in his teens. In the early Golden era of television, Wagner appeared in episodes of *The Adventures of Ozzie and Harriet, Sea Hunt,* and *Dragnet,* to name a few notable shows. In the talent-rich southern California market, Wagner also was a highly successful radio personality, hosting the celebrity interview show *Hollywood on a Silver Platter.* At the height of the show's popularity, it was in syndication to over 1,200 stations coast-to-coast. By his mid 40's, Wagner was an established voice celebrity, but was on the cusp of a major career shift. Disneyland was in his neighborhood, and it was inevitable that Wagner's warm and rich baritone voice would eventually align with Walt Disney Productions.

Wagner, who was an opening day guest at Disneyland on July 17, 1955, did freelance work for Disneyland through its early years, as a guest announcer and narrator for special programs such as Christmas parades. His Disney career officially began in 1970 when he was hired full time as a production consultant. Soon after, he was named the official park announcer. In this role, Wagner created dozens of recordings each day, since many of them were special announcements for a specific event, or to welcome a certain celebrity to the park. To help facilitate a consistent quality of work and for speedy recordings, Disney installed a state-of-the-art recording studio in Wagner's house. Although he lived just a few miles away from Disneyland, Wagner could record all his park announcements from the comfort of his own home. Disneyland also benefited from this arrangement; if an early park closing or late special event announcement needed to be recorded, Wagner could record it and have it ready for immediate use. At the height of his Disney career, he was making recordings for Disneyland, Orlando's Walt Disney World, Tokyo Disneyland, and Euro Disney Resort (now rebranded as Disneyland Paris). Wagner's mellifluous voice, heard at Disney parks on three continents, soothed guests and provided another layer in the Disney experience. He also did voiceover work for Disney's Sunday Night movies, Disney on Ice shows, and various Disney Channel shows. Disneyland officials dubbed him, appropriately enough, the "Walter Cronkite of voice-overs." Wagner even recorded park announcements in the voices of characters such as Mickey Mouse and Donald Duck. "I sometimes think of myself as the eighth dwarf," he recalled, reflecting on the versatility of his voiceover work and studio skills.

Over time, following his retirement in 1991, park announcements needed to be updated, to reflect new parades and attractions, for example. Wagner's original entire monorail recording required changes as new resorts came online as well as new Magic Kingdom elements that needed marketing. His original entire recording is now another entry at Yesterland. However, his iconic "please stand clear of the doors . . ." remains. That audio loop is separate from the in-ride recording and is only played as the monorail doors are preparing to close. Disneyland, similarly, has a vintage Wagner recording still in use to this day. Guests on the Matterhorn will hear his bilingual safety spiel, "remain seated please; permanecer sentados por favor."

Wagner, as a voice professional, did freelance work for other clients outside of Disney. One notable recording is near and dear to Magic Kingdom fans who fly into Orlando International Airport. Upon arrival, travelers board a tram to navigate them to the main terminal. For the short ride, they'll hear an audio recording welcoming them to central Florida. That same reassuring voice used for Disney was now greeting visitors to Orlando's airport. Wagner's comforting tone was the key reason he was hired for the airport project. Said Carolyn Fennell, director of community relations for the Orlando airport: "Jack has a very comfortable voice. It's authoritative without being threatening. One thing you have in an airport is a lot of anxiety. To get people to relax *and* follow instructions is very hard to do."

Wagner relied on one simple ingredient for his recordings. ''I always have to make myself smile when I talk and think friendly thoughts,'' he said. Listening to his park announcements can't help but bring a grin to guests' faces.

Wagner retired in 1991 after vocal cord surgery limited his skills. He died of a heart attack a few years later, on June 16, 1995. However, his warm intonations still in use on the Monorail and Matterhorn have a timeless quality of its own. For his contributions to The Walt Disney Company, Jack Wagner was named a Disney Legend in 2005.

# THE DISNEY EXECUTIVES

# THE MIGHTY JOES

## JOE FOWLER (1990) AND JOE POTTER (1997)

Left photo: June 14, 1958. The christening of the Columbia sailing ship in Disneyland, with Joe Fowler, Walt, Vice Admiral Alfred Richmond (United States Coast Guard) and his wife, Gretchen Campbell Richmond. Right photo: Joe Potter standing before a plot map of the Disney World property, prior to development.

To describe Disneyland as a success would be an understatement by any measure. It recently celebrated the 66th year of operation and hosts roughly sixteen million guests annually. The Disneyland model inspired Disney theme parks in Florida, Europe, and Asia. But Walt, like many times before in his career, had to fight for what he believed would work. The theme park he was proposing was radically new, and Walt, with brother Roy Disney, eventually acquired the capital necessary to create his dream upon 160 acres of orange groves in Anaheim. The construction window, however, was tight. Ground wasn't broken until August 1954, meaning that Disneyland has less than a year to be ready for the scheduled opening of July 17, 1955. Walt had the vision and the dream, but it would take a figurative army to bring it to life. A cadre of animators were recruited into WED Industries (the precursor to today's Walt Disney Imagineering) to conjure attractions and the park layout. The construction was led by Joe Fowler, who originally joined Disney as a naval consultant on the riverboat *Mark Twain* for the Rivers of America.

Joe Fowler, a graduate from the United States Naval Academy and the Massachusetts Institute of Technology (MIT), had a long and distinguished career with the Navy. During

World War II, he ran the operations of all U.S. Navy work in shipyards on the west coast. He formally retired from the Navy in 1948 with the rank of Rear Admiral. He then launched into a second career with Disney that spanned an additional twenty-five years. His first job was construction supervisor of Disneyland. Fowler's organizational prowess was critical to the rapid construction of the park. He recalled the scheduled opening and the pace of the construction: "I had been working right under the limit. I had twenty-five private shipyards (during the war) and by doggie, we had to make dates! There wasn't any two ways about it. That was probably the greatest thing in the world that we opened in July. If we had waited until September when the crowds sloughed off, and so forth, we might never have gotten it off the ground."

One of Walt's most famous quotes is "it's kind of fun to do the impossible." In this vein, Fowler was perhaps a spiritual kin, with his own "can do, can do" catchphrase. Fowler had the drive to bring Disneyland to life and later to run the park as the General Manager. Walt had seemingly impossible ideas for Disneyland, including the now-defunct Tahitian Terrace dinner show. He wanted the waterfall to be able open and the performers would emerge from behind it. Fowler didn't bat an eye and simply said "can do, can do." In 1962, the show premiered with the dual-purpose waterfall, just as Walt wanted.

A lasting tribute to Joe Fowler still stands at Disneyland. Relying on his naval experience, Fowler exhorted to Walt the need for a dry dock on the Rivers of America for maintenance purposes. Fowler won, and the dock was added to the river. It's themed to its Frontierland setting, and is dubbed "Fowler's Harbor."

Fowler's career with the Disney company continued with the Florida project, where he deftly managed his time between three different positions: Senior Vice President, Engineering and Construction for Walt Disney Productions, Chairman of the Board for WED Enterprises, and Director of Construction for Disney's Buena Vista Construction Company. It's here where Fowler would link up with the other indispensable Joe, William "Joe" Potter.

Like Fowler, Joe Potter had a long and distinguished military career before joining Disney. He graduated from the United States Military Academy at West Point and held additional degrees from the National War College and the Massachusetts Institute of Technology. Potter gained invaluable career experience with the military, serving with the Army Corps of Engineers in Nicaragua. During World War II, he worked on the complex logistics involved with the preparation for D Day, the Allied invasion at Normandy. Overall, he had thirty-eight years of experience with the Army and the Corps of Engineers, tackling major construction projects. It was a suitable proving ground for his work at Walt Disney World. After retiring from the Army in 1960, he next worked for the 1964-65 New York World's Fair, directing the construction efforts of corporate and state attractions, leading to his fateful rendezvous with Walt on the Illinois project Great Moments with Mr. Lincoln.

On the strength of his work for the fair, Potter was solicited to work for Disney through a company intermediary. His Disney career began in September 1965 where he was immediately tasked with reviewing the purchased property for the ambitious EPCOT project. Disney's involvement with the mysterious land purchases was unveiled just one month into Potter's tenure. With the project now public, Walt formed a planning group of just three individuals - himself, Disneyland planning veteran and fellow Disney Legend Marvin Davis, and Joe Potter.

Recalled Potter, "One of the things I insisted on was to have a room with sixteen-foot walls at WED. I was tired of making preparations on eight-foot walls. There were only three keys to that room: Marvin's, Walt's and mine. Walt didn't want a committee." The planning room, as seen in the renowned EPCOT film Walt made just prior to his death, features these oversized walls with detailed maps of the property.

Despite the death of Walt in December 1966, plans for a Disney presence in Florida continued. The Magic Kingdom would be built first while Walt's dream of the experimental city was discussed. Potter had the monstrous job of preparing brush land, swamps, and a murky Bay Lake into pristine property. Potter developed a complex series of canals, dubbed Joe's ditches, that drained the swamps and continue today to regulate water levels on property. He also was tasked with installing the infrastructure for the vast location, such as sewer, power, and water treatment plants, all revolutionary at the time.

Potter retired from Disney in 1974, where he earned the moniker "Mr. Disney" in honor of his community outreach efforts in central Florida. His body of work was succinctly expressed by Dick Nunis, former Executive Vice President of Walt Disney World: "Without a Joe Potter there would be no Walt Disney World Today."

The legacy of both Fowler and Potter is present today at Walt Disney World. Guests who traverse the Seven Seas Lagoon to the Magic Kingdom can choose between two magnificent 600 passenger ferryboats, the Admiral Joe Fowler, or the General Joe Potter. Appropriately, each vessel has a plaque honoring its namesake.

# RICHARD IRVINE
## 1990

Magic Kingdom site prep, with "X" for Cinderella Castle circa 1967.
Marty Sklar (left) Welton Becket (center) and Richard Irvine (right),
standing near the "X" that marks the location of Cinderella Castle.

When Walt Disney unveiled Disneyland to the American public in 1955, he set a new standard for theme parks. Roadside carnivals existed before and after, but heavily themed environments didn't exist before Walt, his public company and WED Industries, his privately created band of Imagineers, converted 160 acres of orange groves into the Happiest Place on Earth. Brother Roy worked the logistical challenge of funding the park, while Walt and the Imagineers aimed at a blue sky and conjured up its themed lands and attractions.

Early on, Walt had hired an architectural firm to help with the design of Disneyland, but repeatedly heard the advice that he should be using studio personnel, who would better understand and translate Walt's dream. To head this up, Walt sought studio talent with a background in architecture, and found his man: Richard F. Irvine.

Irvine, brought over from Twentieth Century, arrived at Disney with a background as an artist, classically trained at the Chouinard Art Institute. Additionally, his academic background included studies at Stanford and the University of Southern California in architecture. Irvine's well-deserved reputation for his prior Disney work during the 1940's, as an art director on

*Victory Through Air Power* and *The Three Caballeros*, helped ensure a smooth return. His work at Twentieth Century, also as an art director, included *Miracle on 34th Street*. Back at Disney, Irvine switched from films to theme parks and never looked back.

At WED, Irvine's job was to utilize his art direction and studio experience to translate Walt's thoughts and ideas into a functioning park. He quickly fit in with the other artists and craftsmen as they were developing Disneyland. Engineer Bob Gurr recalled that Richard "was a crucial guy, and he understood the big picture instantaneously . . . whatever Walt started to say, Dick understood it instantly, and could read back to Walt what's going to work, what's not going to work."

Irvine and his Imagineering colleagues worked with Walt on the daunting task of developing layout and contents of Disneyland. "Well, we never stopped making (plans)," Irvine recalled. "We were always in the process of making them. And we'd had many meetings. At that time we were on a forty-eight hour week. We all worked Saturdays. We didn't go on the forty-hour week until after Disneyland was opened. (Walt) was right on top of us. He knew everything that went into that park. He knew where every pipe was. He knew the height of every building."

Like other Imagineers and Disney Legends, Irvine aimed for perfection and personified an attitude of perseverance, that any challenge could be conquered. A key element of Disneyland is the Rivers of America that weaves around Frontierland, New Orleans Square and the now extinct Critter Country, but it was an early engineering challenge - how to properly retain the water within the riverbed. Irvine recollected, "We brought the clay in and used that on the bottom. That's a regular hard pad now. It's like cement. Once we had it that was fine. We didn't know enough to be afraid of anything. We'd tackle anything. Walt would never say 'no,' and you'd get an idea and there was always a way to lick it. That was just a stepping-stone for what was to come later."

Disneyland in 1955 is a far cry from Disneyland as it is today, or even twenty years ago. An early challenge was increasing the park capacity, and the periodic need for wholesale change. Irvine readily admitted that WED "didn't know much about capacity in the early days. We had to learn the hard way that we had under-designed everything, as far as capacity was concerned." As head of planning and development at WED, Irvine had the task of increasing capacity. A fateful weekend in 1956 gave him, Walt, and other Imagineers the opportunity to develop significant changes to Disneyland. A massive rainstorm and its subsequent flooding forced them to hole up in Anaheim, which afforded the opportunity to brainstorm new ideas. Recalled Irvine, "We were all stranded down there overnight for two nights. That was probably one of the most expensive meetings we ever had, because that's when we developed a lot of stuff." As a result, Disneyland received the Skyway in 1956, and later the Disneyland-Alweg Monorail System, the Matterhorn Bobsleds and the Submarine Voyage which opened to public and critical acclaim in 1959.

Following the successful development of Disney's four contributions to the 1964 New York World's Fair, in 1967 Irvine was named Executive Vice President and Chief Operations Officer of WED Enterprises. With over a decade's experience at WED and theme park development, Irvine was ready for the company's next big challenge.

After the death of Walt Disney, plans continued to establish Disney World. Irvine was tasked with the master planning, design and show development of the Florida project, and he implemented some hard-learned lessons, given the luxury of an advanced timeline. For example, he worked with Disney horticulturist Bill Evans to establish the necessary infrastructure for trees and other foliage. Recalling the high cost of mature trees when constructing Disneyland, Irvine said, "The bigger the tree, the more the cost. A big tree would cost five or six, seven hundred dollars, where a small tree would cost fifty dollars or less and grow into a large tree. That's what we learned about it, so that when we went to Florida, we had a tree farm ahead of time. And for three years we grew all the foliage down there for that."

Two years after the successful opening of Walt Disney World, as it was then rebranded, Irvine retired. To honor this talented WED executive, Disney put the Richard F. Irvine riverboat into service on the Rivers of America at the Magic Kingdom. This triple-decker steam paddler has since been rechristened the Liberty Belle and is still in service today. Another Disney watercraft has since taken up his moniker, transporting guests from the Ticket and Transportation Center dock over to the Magic Kingdom.

Richard Irvine passed away in 1976, five days shy of his sixty-sixth birthday. In 1990, The Walt Disney Company honored him as a Disney Legend for his remarkable contributions to WED and the Disney theme parks.

# KAY KAMEN

## 1998

Contemporary guests of the Walt Disney theme parks and the Disney brand are familiar with the gift shop at an attraction exit, or the ubiquitous presence of The Disney Store online, selling all Disney souvenirs. The 'fab five' - Mickey, Minnie, Donald, Pluto and Goofy - are perpetual best-sellers, alongside the bountiful allure of Disney Princess costumes and regalia. Disney merchandise runs the spectrum from simple coloring books to exquisite works of art and diamond-encrusted rings that sell for thousands of dollars. With such a treasure trove of Disney-branded products to choose from, collectors focus on pins,vinly-mation figures or whatever is currently in vogue. But for the true collector of Disneyana merchandise, the 1930's represents when Disney-branded goods became widely available, and extremely lucrative for the Walt Disney Studio. Walt and Roy Disney had one person to thank for the phenomenal success of product placement and marketing: Kay Kamen.

Herman Samuel "Kay" Kamen was born in Baltimore, Maryland on January 27, 1892. His early career was a merchant and an advertising man, a background that would help refine his work marketing Disney characters. His first marketing firm, Kamen-Blair, worked hard to sell and promote retail products such as children's toys and games. Kamen's national reputation was set early on with his successful promotion of the 1920's comedy shorts series *Our Gang*, featuring the likeness of Buckwheat and Pete, the pit bull dog on various products.

Walt and Roy Disney, in the infancy of their company, understood the popularity of Mickey Mouse and the benefits they would reap from his likeness of products. The first licensing contract they signed was with The George Borgfeldt Company who produced Mickey and Minnie Mouse products such as handkerchiefs and plates. However, the quality wasn't up to the Disney standard and a new licensing agreement was sought. In 1932, Kamen, now based out of Kansas City, cold-called Walt about his services. Two days later, Kamen was in Los Angeles for a face-to-face meeting to finish the deal. Kamen squarely sold himself and his services to Walt and Roy and signed a contract to be Disney's sole licensing representative. The terms stipulated that of the first $100,000 in profit, 60% went to Disney and 40% to Kamen. Afterwards, all profits were to be split 50/50. Kamen certainly had a financial incentive to do a sterling job for Disney, and he masterfully performed it. He singlehandedly created the modern marketing campaign for licensing. Tom Tumbusch, publisher of Tomart's Disneyana Update, observed "Kay Kamen invented the whole licensing industry. Not just for Disney, alone; others followed suit."

Kamen's success was built on three principals. First, he understood that the quality of the merchandise he was offering had to match the product that Disney was putting on the screen; Borgfeldt's inferior products were sullying the Disney name. Kamen sold Walt on the notion that Disney would have the final say on the products bearing their intellectual property. Second, he utilized the time-tested secret of marketers - keep in touch with the customer. His primary customers were department stores, the king of retail in his era. Kamen was continuously in touch with his vendors, facilitating two-way communication to determine what products would sell best. Finally, Kamen took that to the final step, preparing marketing material directly for department stores that they could easily display. Kamen did the hard work for the stores, making sales that much easier. For the 1933 Christmas season more than four dozen major department stores in New York City and beyond prominently featured Disney characters in the storefront windows. A year later, the number of stores had grown four-fold.

To help circulate Disney products beyond storefront windows, Kamen created an annual catalog of licensed Disney merchandise. The first few issues, beginning in 1934, featured the primary Disney star, Mickey Mouse. Appropriately enough, it was known as the Mickey Mouse Merchandise Catalog. Later editions went on to feature the growing stable of Disney characters, from lesser-known Silly Symphony players to feature length stars such as Snow White, Doc, Dopey and Pinocchio. Understandably, these catalogs were rebranded as Walt Disney Character Merchandise. Kamen is also credited with the first movie soundtrack, for

*Snow White and the Seven Dwarfs.*

Kamen didn't just benefit Disney. His penchant for quality and marketing saved at least two companies from bankruptcy during the Great Depression. Connecticut-based watch manufacturer Ingersoll Waterbury earned the rights to make the first official Mickey Mouse watch. Fittingly for Walt, it was introduced at the Chicago Century of Progress Exposition in 1933. The watch was such a hit that Ingersoll Waterbury needed to increase the factory personnel tenfold, from 300 to 3,000, to satisfy the market demand for the timepiece. Similarly, the Lionel Corporation, manufacturer of toy trains, saved itself from bankruptcy simply by aligning itself with Disney; its Mickey Mouse wind-up handcar was a blockbuster holiday hit. During these trying financial times, Kamen used the allure of Disney to help sell products. He forged a contract with General Mills for $1 million, giving them the rights to place a smiling Mickey Mouse cut out on the back of cereal boxes.

Tragically, Kamen's life was cut short when he and his wife died in a plane crash on October 28, 1949. All passengers and crew aboard the Air France Lockheed Constellation, flying from Paris to New York with a stopover on Azores, Portugal, perished when the plane crashed on approach to the Santa Maria airport.

Kamen's seventeen-year Disney career bridged the gap from animated Mickey Mouse shorts and Silly Symphonies to the grander scale of feature length films. His career spanned the depths of the Great Depression, the unknown of the World War II years and the post-War boom through the late 1940's. His legacy for Disney is indelible: through 1948, the revenue from Kamen's Disney-licensed products totaled over $100 million. His symbiotic relationship with Disney allowed each to prosper; Walt created timeless characters that connected with the American consumer, and Kamen in turn was able to license Disney characters broadly and smartly for an audience hungry for the product. The profits Disney earned were plowed back into the studio, generating higher quality in Disney films.

For his services to The Walt Disney Company, Kay Kamen was named a Disney legend in 1998.

# CHARLIE RIDGWAY

## 1999

The Walt Disney World resort boasts itself as the Vacation Kingdom of the World. Over 15 million guests visit the four theme parks annually, staying in a Disney resort hotel and participating in a wide variety of recreational activities. Disney fans are fiercely loyal and make many return visits to Orlando. With this background, it should come as no surprise to learn that The Walt Disney Company, including the Walt Disney World resort, has a strong and effective marketing arm, working diligently to attract first time and repeat visitors. In a career that spanned several decades, Disney Legend Charlie Ridgway worked as a masterful publicist for Disney, cultivating critical contacts in the print and television media that helped drive the image of Walt Disney World as the happiest place on earth, and guests to visit it.

Like Walt himself, Ridgway was born in Chicago and grew up in Missouri. He earned a bachelor's degree in journalism from the University of Missouri in 1947 and began his career as a journalist. He soon pursued work in a big city and relocated to Los Angeles in 1952. While working for the Los Angeles Mirror-News, he wrote several articles about the nearby Disneyland theme park under construction. He was there for Disneyland's opening day on July 17, 1955, with press credentials, serving as a witness to the opening of an exciting new era in Disney history. He continued to visit Disneyland, using it as a source of material for feature articles. Through these visits, he met Eddie Meck, Director of Publicity for Disneyland, and developed a strong rapport with him. In 1963, Ridgway joined him in the publicity department, beginning an illustrious Disney career that spanned Anaheim, Orlando, Paris, Tokyo, and Hong Kong.

Ridgway's early Disney career involved working with the press at Disneyland, often arranging photo opportunities. He was fortunate to interact with Walt, frequently staging him for the camera for media events. Ridgway solemnly recalls the last publicity photo of Walt in 1966, posing with Mickey Mouse in front of Sleeping Beauty Castle, just a few months before his untimely passing. That same year, Ridgway was promoted to Disneyland's publicity supervisor.

A few years later, he was promoted again to Publicity Manager for Disney World, in charge of the media and marketing affairs for the massive project in Florida. Ridgway has a fascinating footnote in the history of Walt Disney World. He confesses that he's likely the reason that the Orlando *Sentinel* publicly stated it was Disney secretly buying all the land in central Florida. At the time, Ridgway was handling the year-long promotion of Disneyland's tenth anniversary, dubbed the Tencennial, and was using the company plane to ferry press representatives to Anaheim. In the fall of 1965, the *Sentinel* was contacted after other major markets passed on the offer, and it sent Emily Bavar to California for the event. Upon learning that Orlando press would be in Anaheim, Ridgway was advised by an unnamed senior company officer to "not tell them anything about the Florida Project," which was the first he had heard of it. Ridgway did reply that Walt would be having lunch with the media. Bavar used this opportunity to press Walt about the Florida land purchases. Unprepared, Walt tried to downplay speculation about the company's involvement, but his answers were enough to convince Bavar that Disney was the buyer. "Walt was not a good liar," she later recalled. Several days later, the *Sentinel* ran a front-page headline – "We Say it's Disney" – and the company was forced to publicly announce the plans for what would become Walt Disney World.

After years of development and construction, Walt Disney World was ready to take center stage on October 1st, 1971. Ridgway and his team were prepared, but he does recall the frantic activities leading up to that day. A portion of the Polynesian Resort was designated for the press, but on the eve of opening day, it was barely ready, lacking carpeting, wallpaper, phones, and desks! When Ridgway arrived the next morning for work, the room was fully furnished and ready for action.

Ridgway hatched one of the more impressive ideas at the Magic Kingdom. A special parade was developed to celebrate Donald Duck's fiftieth anniversary, in 1984. During a brainstorming session, Ridgway suggested they get fifty ducks to march behind Donald in the parade. To his surprise, he learned that it could be done, provided the ducklings were hatched in the presence of Donald himself, to immediately bond. As the ducklings grew, they spent every day with Donald, learning to follow him on cue. When it was time for the parade, the ducks were all prepared, and Disney magic followed.

Ridgway had a direct role in creating and then marketing Epcot. He made countless trips overseas on behalf of the company to cultivate relationships with foreign governments to lay the framework for the World Showcase pavilions. On October 1st, 1979, three years before the park opened, He staged an elaborate public relations photo of the groundbreaking ceremony, with an eighteen story, two-dimensional recreation of Spaceship Earth and a massive dump truck that proudly displayed an "EPCOT Center" banner, as the park was originally named. Three years later on opening day, Ridgway and his team helped orchestrate publicity of the new park in a fashion perfectly suited for one of the park's central tenets – communication. Satellite television technology, unavailable for the opening of Disneyland or the Magic Kingdom, was the latest tool available for marketing. Ridgway arranged for a satellite uplink for local news station reporters from around the country. They could do a live report directly from the park and have it beamed to their hometown. With the aid of dozens of news stations reporting 'locally,' awareness of Epcot's opening reached an amazing 90%, surveys showed.

Ridgway's next major park assignment was the Disney-MGM Studios park, now known as Disney's Hollywood Studios. After the initial surge in attendance, visitor numbers dropped and required a PR boost. Ridgway and his team created the "Star Today" marketing plan, in which each week a Hollywood star would be featured at the park, even available for guest question and answer sessions. Luminaries such as Michael J. Fox, Andy Griffiths and Angela Lansbury were featured, and the parks reputation and attendance began to climb.

North America wasn't big enough for Ridgway. He spent a year in Paris setting up the publicity department for Euro Disney, since renamed to Disneyland Paris. He was also instrumental in the publicity of Disney's park in Tokyo and Hong Kong

Ridgway retired from Disney in 1994 but remained on as a consultant for the company for several additional years. He recalls, "I witnessed the creation of eleven Disney parks, two Downtown Disneys, thirty hotels, two campgrounds and four water parks in the U.S., Japan, France and China. I wrote press releases about all of them and was there for most of those openings." Appropriately enough, he's honored with a window on Main Street, U.S.A. that reads: "Ridgway and Company. Public Relations. Charles Ridgway, Press Agent. 'No event too small.'"

Ridgway was named a Disney Legend in 1999. He passed away on December 24, 2016.

# PIXAR ANIMATION STUDIOS

Since 1995, with the release of the critical and commercial hit *Toy Story*, Pixar Animation Studios and The Walt Disney Company have enjoyed a prosperous relationship together. Pixar has elegantly crafted unique and wholly original animated features entirely through the new medium of computer graphics imagery (CGI), relying on pixels and computers rather than traditional ink and paint. The animation process may be different, but the creative workflow remains the same. Craft and refine a heartwarming story, populate it with relatable and endearing characters and fold in a sentimental musical score. All combined, Pixar's multiple cinematic releases, with the *Toy Story* franchise serving as anchor, have yielded a dozen Academy Awards. Story and voice artists, composers, and a guiding hand to nurture the process all come together. It's only fitting that several recipients of the Disney Legends award earned this coveted award for their contributions to Pixar.

There's a simple motto at Pixar, both when it was an independent studio, whose films were distributed by Disney, and today as a Disney-owned studio: "story is king." Before a script is completed, the story and its characters, plot and settings must be coaxed into form. Joe Ranft (2006) masterfully served at Pixar as a story artist. Formally trained at CalArts, alongside Pixar co-founder John Lasseter, Ranft honed his animation skills at Disney under the tutelage of Eric Larson, one of Walt's Nine Old Men. Ranft migrated to Pixar and helped to define the early films as a story supervisor. His intuitive approach helped Pixar establish its identity early on, with back-to-back hits of *Toy Story* and *A Bug's Life*. Recalled Pete Docter, director of *Monsters Inc.* and *UP*, "Joe was really a major part of Pixar's soul. He was one of the key players who made all the films what they are." Ranft was tragically killed in 2005 in an automobile accident while *Cars* was in production, leaving his future contributions to Pixar unfulfilled. Ranft himself best summed up his work as a story artist - "I have the notion that there's a story there that wants to be told, and you're just trying to find out what it is. And you go from trying to lead it to listening and letting it lead you."

Pixar relies on veteran Hollywood talent to bring its animated characters to life. Three actors are now Disney Legends honorees on the strength of their voice artist work for Pixar: Tim Allen (1999), Billy Crystal (2013) and John Goodman (2013). Allen brought the self-absorbed space cadet Buzz Lightyear of the *Toy Story* franchise to life and reprised the same role in the affiliated shorts such as *Hawaiian Vacation*. Allen's ties to Disney run deeper than just Pixar; he parlayed his stand-up comic fame into Tim Taylor on Disney-owned ABC's *Home Improvement*, which ran from 1991 to 1999. His Disney credentials also include portraying Kris Kringle in *The Santa Clause* films, and his narrated DisneyNature's 2012 theatrical release, *Chimpanzee*.

The voice of Buzz Lightyear was originally offered to Crystal, who infamously declined.

He wasted no time accepting the next Pixar role offered to him, the eternally optimistic one-eyed wonder Mike Wazowski of *Monsters, Inc.* and *Monsters University.* Crystal is a multi-decade veteran of television, film, and stage, yet he says Wazowski is "my favorite character I've ever played." Outside of Pixar, Crystal has hosted the Academy Awards show on ABC nine times. Wazowski's blue and green furry friend from the *Monsters* films is James "Sully" Sullivan, voiced by the full-throated Goodman, who accurately captures Sully's swagger and style. Like Allen, Goodman is also a veteran of ABC television and other Disney films. For over ten seasons, he portrayed everyman Dan Conner on *Roseanne* and its spinoff, *The Connors.* His Disney feature animation credits include "Big Daddy" La Bouff in *The Princess And The Frog,* Baloo in *Jungle Book* 2 and the irresistible Pacha in *The Emperor's New Groove.*

All films need a musical score and perhaps a toe-tapping number or two to enhance the emotional arc of the story. Pixar is blessed to have Randy Newman (2007) as a frequent collaborator. He began his musical career crafting irresistible pop tunes. His catchy *I Love L.A.*, a summer ode to the southern California lifestyle, still resonates today. He shifted his talents to the broader canvas of musical scores which led to the coveted job of the *Toy Story*

soundtrack. His Pixar credits include the *Toy Story* franchise, *A Bug's Life*, both *Monsters* films and *Cars*. Additionally, he penned ample songs from these movies. The *Toy Story* films yielded such hits as "You've Got a Friend in Me," "Strange Things" and "We Belong Together," all which featured his distinctive, husky baritone voice. Perhaps his most poignant song is Jessie's hauntingly sublime "When She Loved Me," sung by Sarah McLachlan. Newman received multiple Academy Award nominations for his Pixar work and finally took home the coveted Oscar for Best Original Song for his single "If I Didn't Have You" from *Monsters, Inc.*

Ultimately, Pixar Animation would not exist today, nor would it have an unbelievable string of hit films to its credit, had it not been for Steve Jobs (1993), the original benefactor and CEO of the young company who believed it was capable of truly great things. Without his support through the lean early years, it's no stretch to suggest that Pixar, despite the technical and artistic wizards on board, owes its success to him.

Jobs is best known for the Apple Computer Company he co-founded in 1976 which launched the first truly personal computer, the Apple ][ and then the MacIntosh, with its then revolutionary graphical interface. Jobs was forced out of Apple in 1985 over a boardroom dispute. This catalytic event allowed Jobs the personal freedom to explore new arenas, including purchasing from George Lucas his Industrial Light and Magic entity that eventually became Pixar. Jobs eventually returned to Apple and developed the iPod, a portable music player and the iPhone and iPad, mobile devices for an increasingly untethered crowd. Pixar, however, never strayed far off his radar. He trusted Ed Catmull and John Lasseter to provide the necessary wizardry to bring CGI films to life but still relied on his instincts to guide the entire process. Jobs once stated, regarding the various products Apple developed, "people don't know what they want until you show it to them." The same concept can apply to Pixar, which showed the world that animation can be created by new means and methods, as long as the story and characters resonate.

Jobs passed away in 2011, leaving behind a rich legacy at both Apple and Pixar. Lasseter accepted Jobs' Disney Legends award in 2013 on behalf of Steve's family and shared his personal experiences with Jobs. He recalled an early conversation during the production of *Toy Story*: "'John, when I make the computers at Apple, the lifespan is about three years; five years, it's a doorstop. If you do your job right, what you and Pixar create can last forever.' And he's right. Name another movie that was released in 1937 that is watched today and will be watched as much in the future, as *Snow White and the Seven Dwarfs*."

The Pixar and Disney families are deeply connected to each other, so it's only fitting that the Disney Legends program honors those who helped shape Pixar into what it is today.

# THE RENAISSANCE PLAYERS

Some Disney Legends can't be neatly defined by a single field of work. Instead, their contributions span multiple disciplines. These are the artisans of The Walt Disney Company, whose skills allowed for a renaissance of growth for the company.

# Marc and Alice Davis

## (1989 AND 2004)

Disney Legends, worthy of their title, make deep and lasting contributions to The Walt Disney Company. They come from all walks of life and have disparate backgrounds that channel their creativity to the silver screen and theme parks. It's the rare and wonderful opportunity when they can share their personal and professional lives together. Such is the case with Marc Davis and Alice Estes Davis. Each brought their personal artistry to Disney and shared a fulfilling life together.

If Marc Davis isn't a household name of Disney fans, then his work certainly is. Described by Walt as his "Renaissance Man," Davis' animation work spans over twenty years, and he's given life to some of Disney's most iconic animated women, both heroes and villains. He seamlessly made the transition to WED Industries where he plussed existing Disneyland attractions and put his signature stamp on newer classics.

Marc Davis was born in Bakersfield California in 1913. His father was in the oil business, and the Davis family frequently relocated to the next prospect. As a result, Marc attended over twenty schools before he graduated. He considered this an asset rather than a liability; he later recalled, "I discovered that I could amuse myself when I was lonely by drawing. But I also learned that I could go anywhere and meet anyone. I had so much experience in the world by the time I was through high school." With his strong interest and natural ability in art, Marc furthered his artistic ambition through art school. He refined his education by spending hours at nearby zoos sketching animals, carefully studying their physiology. This would be a key factor in his Disney career.

With resume in hand, Marc applied to Walt Disney Productions, as the company was known at the time, and was an immediate hire, working on *Snow White and the Seven Dwarfs*. His early animation stood out, particularly the dancing sequence between Snow White and two dwarfs, one atop another. He worked next on *Bambi*, excelling with his knowledge of animal anatomy, primarily on Flower, the skunk.

Marc's animation contributions of iconic characters earned him, humorously, the distinction of being a ladies' man. In sequence, he animated Cinderella, Alice from *Alice in Wonderland*, Tinker Bell, both Maleficient and Aurora from *Sleeping Be*auty and finally his masterpiece, Cruella De Vil from *One Hundred and One Dalmatians*. In this timeframe, he taught evening animation courses at the Chouinard Art Institute and had the serendipitous fortune to have Alice Estes as one of his students. Marc sought out her expertise in clothing design when he needed a special dress for the live-action reference model for *Sleeping Beauty*. A romance between Marc and Alice followed and led to their marriage in 1956. Alice Davis, also a California native, was born in 1929. She attended the Chouinard Art Institute hoping to enroll in animation but given the backlog of applicants in the male-dominated industry, she accepted the only opening available, in costume design. Following graduation, she went on to become a noted lingerie designer. She returned to Chouinard for night classes in animation, setting up the fateful encounter with Marc. Walt met the young couple one evening at dinner and, after learning of Alice's skills as a fashion designer, gave her the opportunity to work for Disney designing costumes for live-action films.

Marc's Disney career was about to take a major turn. With a keen eye for staging and set design, he was tasked with Disney's next big endeavor. Disneyland was just a few years old, and Walt was ready for a fresh set of eyes to review it. Marc was sent to take a "good, hard, critical look" at the Frontierland attraction Mine Train Through Nature's Wonderland. He reported back that it has no gags or clear story and pitched ideas to Imagineering for adding animal humor. His background in animal physiology allowed him to speak authoritatively. With this under his belt, Marc was next assigned to update the Jungle Cruise, which in its first iteration didn't have the present-day humor it's now famous for. Marc injected much of that into it, notably the classic elephant pool scene.

Walt's next major project was developing four unique Disney-style attractions for the 1964 New York World's Fair. Both Marc and Alice had the special opportunity to work together, notably on "it's a small world" (in its deliberate use of lower casing) and Walt Disney's

Carousel of Progress. On the former, Alice created the costumes for the dolls of the world in the Mary Blair-designed attraction. Alice brought a sharp eye for detail, noting that Blair's design of red fur hats for the English dolls was historically inaccurate, and instead fashioned the costume correctly with black fur. For Alice, a child of the Great Depression, it was an exuberant feeling to have been a part of creating the world's most exclusive doll collection. On the latter, Marc's whimsical style shined brightly, notably the brief scene of Uncle Orville in the bathtub. Alice was responsible for period-specific clothing.

Marc and Alice would again collaborate on another timeless Disney classic, Pirates of the Caribbean. Alice did the costume designs for the buccaneers, recalling that she "went from sweet little children to dirty old men overnight." Marc's broad sketches of pirates in action were brought vividly to life. His scenes were created as staged sets, and instantly readable, necessary for the continuous passage of guests through the attraction yet layered with enough density to assure repeatability. He recalled, "When we showed the auction scene from Pirates to Walt, I said, 'I'm sorry - I think there is too much to see at one time here.' Walt said, 'My God, that's great! We do so much business down here, that means that the next time people come through, they'll see something they haven't seen before!'"

Grandpa Marc, as the tombstone outside the Haunted Mansion states, was a key contributor to Disneyland's other mysterious and spooky classic attraction. Marc's playful style shines brightly on the elaborate graveyard scene that concludes the attractions.

Both Pirates of the Caribbean and the Haunted Mansion were recreated for Walt Disney World's Magic Kingdom, albeit with notable differences. For the new park, Marc had a daring and detailed new attraction, the Western River Expedition, that he designed for the outer edge of Frontierland. However, it was never realized as intended. Pirates of the Caribbean, opened in 1973, and Big Thunder Mountain Railroad, opened in 1980, occupy the plot where Western River Expedition was anticipated. Marc did create a Magic Kingdom original classic, the Country Bear Jamboree, which began its development in the mid 1960s for the unfulfilled Mineral King Ski Resort. The project was shifted to Florida and became an instant opening day hit.

With significant contributions to Disney films and theme park attractions to their names, Marc and Alice Davis retired from The Walt Disney Company in 1978. Marc passed away in 2000, and Alice remained active in the Disney community before her death in 2022. They have been memorialized on Main Street, U.S.A with windows, appropriately enough side-by-side. For their significant contributions to The Walt Disney Company, Marc Davis was named a Disney Legend in 1989, and Alice Davis in 2004.

# Ub Iwerks
## 1989

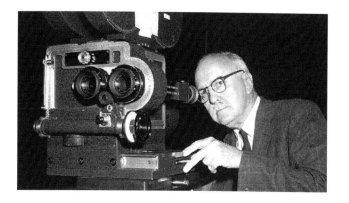

The Disney Legends program, established in 1987, serves to acknowledge and honor the many individuals whose imagination, talents and dreams have created the Disney magic. Ubbe Iwwerks, a gifted animator and visual effects master, was bestowed with this honor in 1989. Iwwerks, who later shortened his unique name to Ub Iwerks, was born in Kansas City in 1901. Kansas City was fertile ground for animators in the early 20th century, and this is where Ub first met Walt Disney in 1917, the first of three critical intersections throughout their careers. They worked together briefly for an ad agency and then formed their own company, the Iwwerks-Disney Commercial Artists, for freelance work. They continued together at the Kansas City Film Ad Company where they experimented with film animation. Walt and Ub wanted to push this new medium further and incorporated a new company for this purpose: Laugh-O-gram Films. Their work was artistically rewarding but commercially unsuccessful and in 1923, Laugh-O-Gram filed for bankruptcy. After that, Walt made his fateful trip to Los Angeles. For five years together in Kansas City, Walt and Ub formed an intimate bond of artistry, technician, and showmanship.

Walt Disney, with brother Roy, established The Disney Brothers Cartoon Studio in October 1923 and began working on the Alice Comedies series, a rudimentary hybrid of live-action and animation. Walt convinced Ub to join him in 1924, and their second career intersection began, this time with remarkable results. Ub and Walt created a plucky and popular new character, Oswald the Lucky Rabbit. Walt lost the rights to Oswald and most of his animators to Charles Mintz, the Oswald distributor who technically owned the rights to the animated character. Ub remained loyal to Walt and together they created the iconic Mickey Mouse. Ub was a prolific illustrator on the Mickey Mouse shorts, almost single-handedly animating the early cartoons at up to 700 drawings a day. Mickey Mouse made history in 1928 when he debuted in *Steamboat Willie,* the first animation to feature synchronized sound. Ub played a critical role in providing the musical conductor a unique working copy of the cartoon that enabled the orchestral recording to match the animation. Ub continued his artistic deftness for Walt with his work on a new line of cartoons known as the Silly Symphonies, starting with the ground-breaking *Skeleton Dance.* The prodigious work of Ub Iwerks with Oswald, Mickey Mouse and Silly Symphonies allowed the Disney Brothers Studios, later renamed to Walt Disney Productions and then later to The Walt Disney Company, to flourish and grow. It's not an exaggeration to suggest that Ub shares equal credit with Walt for laying the foundation for the company. With his artistic name made, Iwerks left in 1930 to form his own animation studio.

After ten years of working on his own, further exploring animation boundaries and tinkering with the mechanical elements of filming, Ub returned to Walt Disney Productions for his third and most critical career intersection with Walt. He began work in the Production Control Department and made immediate contributions to *Fantasia,* in which he orchestrated the scene of Mickey Mouse shaking the hand of conductor Leopold Stokowski. In *Dumbo's* pink elephant sequence, Ub created a new color separation process that allowed for a variety of eye-popping hues. For *Bambi,* he created a realistic rain effect by combining a filmed waterfall with animation.

To better utilize Ub's increasingly technical skills, in 1943 Walt named him the head of the newly created Disney Optical Printing Department. Ub came to the rescue of Walt's new True-Life Adventure films, by creating a new process in which 16mm prints could be enlarged to 35mm for theater use. This "wet gate" process removed the inherit problem of scratches on the film during enlargement. Ub's growing role now would be technical work on Disney's expansion into live-action films. He enhanced a color separation system which uses mattes with live-action filming to better control color balance, density, and contrast. Ub also improved upon the sodium vapor process, like contemporary green-screen filming, which allows actors to be filmed in studio and merged with background mattes in post-production.

For any Hollywood studio to grow, cost-saving measures need to be present. In this regard, Ub made a significant contribution to the animation process, beginning with the classic *One Hundred and One Dalmatians.* Xerox photocopying technology had arrived at the business world, and Ub modified it to apply to the animation world. He created the Xerographic Fusing Apparatus and the Xerographic Developing Apparatus that allowed for the animators' work to be directly applied to translucent animation celuloids, often known simply as cels. This bypassed the laborious inking process. Fellow Disney Legend Floyd Norman recalls Ub's contribution: "With smaller crews and a greatly compressed production schedule, *One Hundred and One Dalmatians* was completed in a fraction of the time it took to create *Sleeping Beauty.* That meant a huge cost savings and a new lease on life for Disney's Animation Department."

Ub's best recognized Disney film accomplishment, perhaps, is the "jolly holiday" sequence from *Mary Poppins,* featuring Bert and Mary whimsically dancing with animated farm animals and penguins. It's not the first time live-action and animation have been merged, but Ub's traveling-matte process allowed for the animated characters to move from the background freely and seamlessly to the foreground within the scene. Ub made a notable contribution outside of Disney, when he provided special effects for Alfred Hitchcock's *The Birds.* Ub filmed multiple scenes of birds flying via the sodium vapor matte process, and when layered they created the frightening aviary attacks.

Ub didn't limit his technical prowess to the Disney film department. He contributed to WED Enterprises, the precursor of today's Imagineers. First, he created the Circarama film concept that debuted at Disneyland in 1955, offering park guests a 360-degree film experience. He later enhanced the process with Circle-Vision, which removed blind spots from the multiple cameras used in filming. For Disney's contributions to the 1964-65 World's Fair, Ub created the photoelectric control system for Great Moments with Mr. Lincoln to allow the Audio-An-imatronic president to operate. Lincoln was the progenitor to the Hall of Presidents, for which Ub developed lighting and film effects.

Ub's fingerprints are on two of Disney's beloved attractions. For the Haunted Mansion, he developed the process of projecting a face onto a static object, giving the impression of life. Guests will know this as the disembodied Madame Leota crystal ball and the singing busts. For Pirates of the Caribbean, Ub created an electrical circuit to allow light bulbs to flicker, simulating the natural appearance of candles.

For his technical accomplishments, Ub was twice presented with an Academy Award. His first trip to the podium was in 1960 for a Technical Achievement Award for "the design of an improved optical printer for special effects and matte shots." His second Oscar was in 1965 for the "conception and perfection of techniques for Color Traveling Matte Composite Cinematography" utilized in *Mary Poppins.*

Walt Disney himself had high praise for Ub's skills. Late in their careers, Walt recollected that Ub was a "natural engineering genius and one of the nicest guys that ever lived. He can do anything." The Walt Disney company is indebted to Ub Iwerks' many accomplishments, and he is worthy of the title of Disney Legend.

# INDEX

The following is a complete listing of Disney Legend honorees through 2023. Names in bold indicate those who are profiled in Disney Legends, Volume 1 along with their respective page numbers. Other individuals will be profiled in future volumes.

Made in the USA
Middletown, DE
17 October 2023

40990865R00075